Isla
Summ

Island Summers

Memories of a Norwegian Childhood

TILLY CULME-SEYMOUR

BLOOMSBURY

LONDON · NEW DELHI · NEW YORK · SYDNEY

First published in Great Britain 2013

Copyright © 2013 by Tilly Culme-Seymour

Maps by Tim Makower

The moral right of the author has been asserted.

The quotation on page ix is taken from *Letters Written During a Short
Residence in Sweden, Norway and Denmark* by Mary Wollstonecraft.

Bloomsbury Publishing Plc
50 Bedford Square
London WC1B 3DP

www.bloomsbury.com

Bloomsbury Publishing, London, New Delhi, New York and Sydney
A CIP catalogue record for this book is available from the British Library

ISBN 978 1 4088 1213 6

10 9 8 7 6 5 4 3 2 1

Typeset by Hewer Text UK Ltd, Edinburgh
Printed and bound in Great Britain by CPI Group (UK) Ltd, Croydon CR0 4YY

MIX
Paper from
responsible sources
FSC
www.fsc.org
FSC® C020471

Plate section picture credits: Page 12, bottom © Charlotte Baker Wilbraham.
Pages 14, 15, 16 © Jason Lowe.

To Caroline Elizabeth Peto Bennett

In Memoriam Roald Hellenes: 1933–2012

CONTENTS

CONTENTS

Indeed, I am led to conclude, that the sweetest summer in the world, is the northern one.

Mary Wollstonecraft

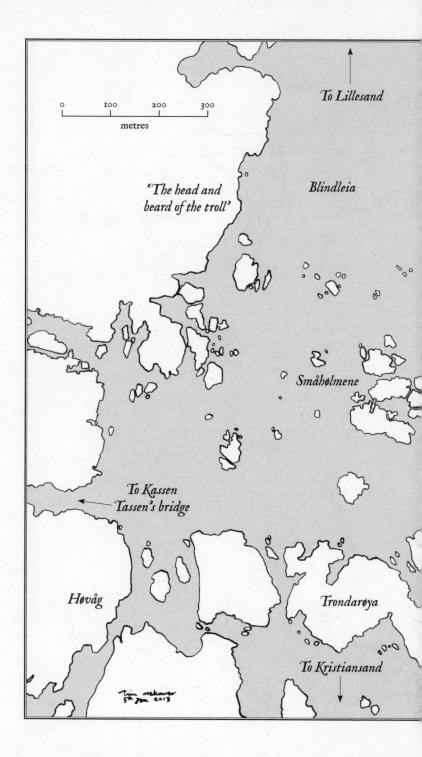

To Lillesand

Blindleia

'The head and
beard of the troll'

Småhølmene

To Kassen
Tassen's bridge

Høvåg

Trondarøya

To Kristiansand

0   100   200   300
metres

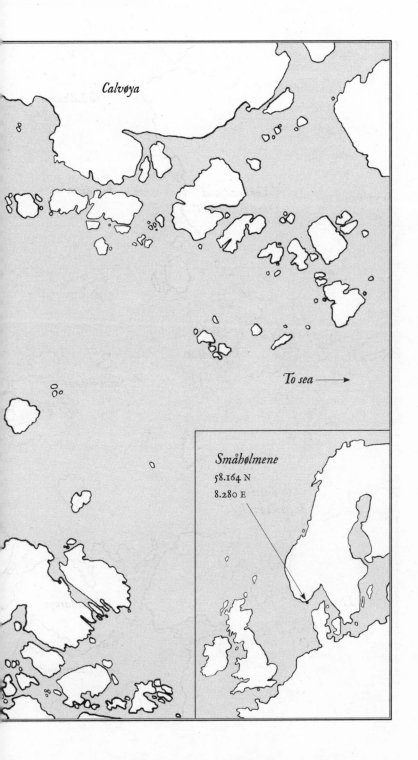

Calvøya

To sea ⟶

Småhølmene
58.164 N
8.280 E

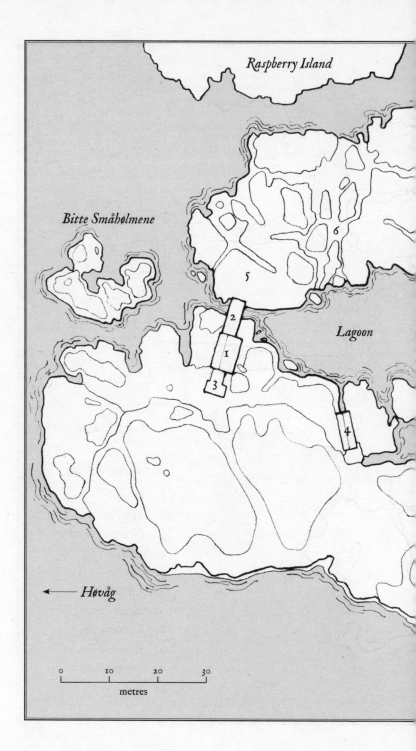

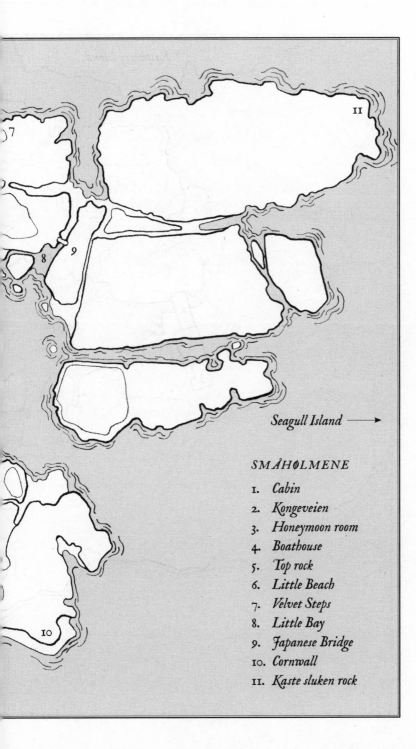

Seagull Island ⟶

SMÅHØLMENE

1. *Cabin*
2. *Kongeveien*
3. *Honeymoon room*
4. *Boathouse*
5. *Top rock*
6. *Little Beach*
7. *Velvet Steps*
8. *Little Bay*
9. *Japanese Bridge*
10. *Cornwall*
11. *Kaste sluken rock*

The Island

My grandmother bought the island. The year was 1947 and she was thirty-three, a couple of years older than I am now. She built on it a two-storey wooden cabin, with three bedrooms, a sitting-room, a galley kitchen and an outside loo, which she and her four children decorated with postcards to occupy themselves on a rainy day. Sea lapped against the rocks beneath the bridge, on which the water chamber was poised, as though standing on stilts. Sea galloped through the lagoon-mouth, across the lagoon and up over the *brygge*, inciting the boats to tug and scrape against their moorings. Sea dashed the outlying skerries and swirled into a horizon of thick mist and hoar. Rain clattered on the roof tiles and streaked the window-panes. Damp curled the edges of the postcards around the door, hooked open to let in light for them to work by. The island season was principally from midsummer to the end of August, and the day, the exposure, called into question whether even that window could safely be called summer. Half a century on we are still a family of

Norwegian islanders – an identity that demands contingent beliefs in both the virtues of wet weather and the sweetness of fair skies.

The island is on the south coast of Norway. It is called Småhølmene, pronounced 'Smor-hol-min-a', the accented 'å' losing the original crisp vowel sound we know in English, and becoming more of a muddy 'oh'. On the island of Småhølmene much of the day is devoted to the collection and preparation of food. For food makes activity and activity is invaluable on an island. We go fishing in the dawn and on midnight crabbing expeditions; we spend afternoons picking berries and hunting for mushrooms; we climb for mussels on still days and collect windfall apples on wild ones: all these have value and importance over the long summer weeks. Then there is the quiet pleasure of scrubbing potatoes, legs dangling over the *brygge*, stopping every now and then to rinse muddy hands in the clean salt water. We go thieving for gulls' eggs and collect juniper berries from high outcrops, as well as sorrel and samphire – sea asparagus – which grows near the ledge known as the Velvet Steps.

The Velvet Steps is a ledge about a foot beneath the surface of the sea covered in soft greenish weed, barnacles and starfish. From here, my Norwegian grandmother Mor-mor would glide into the water with a bag between her teeth to collect wild raspberries from the island opposite, her big black poodle Cheri swimming by her side. The channel to Raspberry Island, where the sweetest fruit is found, though not more than thirty metres wide, is deeper and darker than the lagoon. It is colder and rougher too, fed by the open sea. Such missions were not to faze Mor-mor; for her it was all a part of the great adventure of island foraging.

The first and only photograph of my grandmother and me together depicts a quintessential Småhølmene scene. We are sitting on a chequered blue *dyne*, propped against the rock in front of the kitchen door. I used to think a gigantic snake had curled into that rock, for running down from its summit is lodged a deep, spiralling imprint, very wormlike and forbidding. I am sandwiched between Mor-mor, her face concealed by a mane of butterscotch-coloured hair, and Dordie, my next sister up, her pale bare legs sticking out across the *dyne*. I am holding a Puffin picture book with one hand, while the other rests innocently in Mor-mor's grasp. Beside her on the granite are a cup of half-finished tea and a cereal bowl with a knife balanced across it. One can somehow tell that it is a sunny-windy day, the kind of day you cannot help but appreciate being on the island, when the company of a good book along with the comfort of camp provisions and something soft to cushion the hard rock are ingredients for an overwhelming sense of content and well-being.

The island cabin was built by Mor-mor over the autumn of 1948, resurrecting memories of pre-war island life, and thirty-five years later, in 1983, I had my first Småhølmene summer. I might never have made it to the island at all if Mor-mor had been given her head and had me siphoned off on a childless cousin when I was an infant. Explaining herself after, she would say that she felt a sixth child, and a girl to boot, was too much for my already overstretched Mamma, who thankfully rebelled from the maternity ward. Perhaps my grandmother wanted in some weird way to make history repeat itself. Mor-mor herself had been abandoned by a cavalier mother and a charming but selfish father, who fled to America when his wife decamped. Instead, she was raised by a kindly uncle, who saw to it that she was on an equal footing with his own daughter, with all the same privileges of dress and education. Though she met with much love and understanding, her own parents had disappointed her. She was a dependant who must in gratitude to her uncle suppress the yearning within her to call something her own.

I did not begrudge Mor-mor her plot. Rather it was an indulgence to try to imagine the other life she had mapped out for me with my distant Norwegian cousins; to imagine who I might have become, placed among relations so far removed that I never met them once through the whole course of my life. I used the real-life tales of Mor-mor's early years to help me along, animated them by putting myself in her shoes: walking up the imposing driveway of an unknown mansion in the outskirts of Oslo, wearing a best prune-coloured velvet coat with a matching muffler and bonnet; being given a beautiful china doll by a new Pappa and Mamma and dropping it pettishly on the floor, smashing it on the marble. Then I sympathised with my grandmother and thought the best of her – perhaps as Sosse, the daughter of her adoptive household, might have done, inspecting her curious young cousin.

Mor-Mor translates as 'Mother's mother'. Mor-mor is my mother's mother. The Norwegian name is pronounced with a great rolling of 'r's, but among Mor-mor's grandchildren, who have been educated mostly in England, she is known simply as 'Mud-mud', or 'Muddy'. When my uncle Christopher had three daughters, Mor-mor had become a Far-mor, to mean 'Father's mother'. Yet the family's parliament of women decreed she was always only Mor-mor.

Over the last century my family has been strong in the female line. This is the story of three of its formidable women: Mor-mor, my mother and me. Mor-mor was a woman of considerable vision and resourcefulness. How else to interpret her determined acquisition of a rock nobody else would have thought to stop at for long, still less to live on? Mor-mor was the originator, the ideas maker, the spur. Mamma was – is – the custodian. She has accepted her eccentric inheritance with grace and forbearance. I, her last daughter, chanced upon an unlikely legacy. My own story comes from an angle of accidental privilege, the impetus of the great good luck that brought me to Småhølmene.

I first grasped how powerful continuity for its own sake could be when watching Mamma repeating Mor-mor's island ways. There were rites and superstitions which went against sense. She might be halfway up her annual climb of the steepest rock above the boathouse, with a handhold of wet moss, pause, and say dreamily, 'Mummy used to do this to make sure she came back the year after next.' I used to think her mad. Experience has taught me that I too am in shackles to the past and nowhere more so than the island kitchen. Even Mor-mor's more flamboyant dishes have a romantic appeal. Her cookery related to the landscape, the place and the people around her. I hope in this respect I am a true upholder of the old regime.

Child of fortune that I was, I always saw the island as horseshoe-shaped; with two long arms of rock curving around a lagoon, protecting it from the beat of the sea so that it remains tranquil and warmish on even the most blustery day. The horseshoe is a talisman nailed right-ways outside a door but brings bad luck the wrong way round. Well, the island was for me a cup filled with such magic and adventure, I never imagined it could swing on its axis and empty of joy. Today it has almost done so, as the threat of what will happen to Småhølmene in years to come looms large.

I am a cookery writer by trade. My memory is, as for many people, strongly linked to taste and smell. The island is the setting for some of my most cherished childhood food memories: simple pleasures like a fish pulled wriggling from the sea and fried in butter minutes later; or the welcome salt hit of bacon cooked with tomatoes after a cold swim; or *bløtkake*, a cake so unctuous that when my mother sat on it, cooling under a rug in the passenger seat of the family estate, such a quantity of cream spurted out as to mark the car's leather upholstery for ever. It has meant that I relish hearing of Mor-mor's own tastes, for instance her love of black pepper, which led her to exclaim one day, 'Why, I am a pepper troll!' Her eccentricities were expressed through food. She told anybody who asked for a length of her beloved liquorice that it was tyre rubber, thus avoiding having to share it with them. Mountaineering, she sucked on the stones of plums, turning them over with her tongue while crossing the rugged terrain, rather as a concentrating pupil might stick theirs out while solving a puzzling algebra equation. On such expeditions, her brood of four children would be left behind somewhere convenient, nursing oranges and a carefully packaged bundle of white sugar lumps through which to drink the juice. Even her death seems in a macabre way linked to food, for the morning she died she devoured a plate of scrambled eggs with all the relish of having stolen them from under the nose of the cook.

Mor-mor's end came four years after my arrival, at Easter, 1985. Through absence one might still build the scaffolding of friendship, or kinship, and it is the more remarkable that it is by inclination alone, in silent dialogue with the past, that a living person can unearth their dead. Mor-mor's very absence awakened my curiosity. I could not hear enough about her habits and tastes, her character – appearing by all accounts handsomer held at a distance, seen through the mists as it were – and began to wonder what aspect of that character, those tastes and habits, filtered through to me, her youngest grandchild.

Småhølmene brought out the poet in Mor-mor. Mamma's diary writing and letters take inspiration from it as well. In one, sent to me before I embarked on a solo trip to the island, she describes having what she calls 'a rebirth of memories'. She paints Mor-mor in vivid sweeps, her big character lifting off the page blemishes and all. This alone would be interesting for me as a virtual stranger to my grandmother, but I recognise aspects of myself and the author, Mamma's, self-portrait too; the fierce rower, the keen provider – it captures all of us on the island. When Mamma writes 'rebirth' she means, I think, that Mor-mor is incarnate in her, in me. Her portrait is *our* portrait.

Yet in all my detective work what have I to go on but stories, some of them probably wildly inaccurate, as stories will become when left to themselves to prove over the years. Of course all that time and mulling makes them of good vintage. Take Småhølmene. It must seem very privileged for a family to own a whole island. Today it would be the preserve of the super-rich, a luxury retreat for the idle and leisured. But Mor-mor struck it lucky when one summer's afternoon she saw the rocky outline of Småhølmene for the first time, for she had pluck and was the visionary sort of person who can make something magical out of very little. Mamma swears Mor-mor bought Småhølmene in exchange for a mink coat.

Småhølmene means Small Isles. It is, as it sounds, a collection of tiny islands, like Canna, Rùm, Eigg and Muck, the other Small Isles, in the Scottish Inner Hebrides. There is Bringebærholmen, or Raspberry Island, dotted with wild raspberry canes; Måkeholmen, Seagull Island, ruled by a colony of hostile seabirds; then the smooth grey contours of Elefantholmen, Elephant Island, lying to the south.

The *hytte* stands on the central island, which gives us a protected feeling as though the outer isles were battlements and the cabin our fortress. History tells of the natural defence provided by the thousands of isles and skerries of the districts of *Vest-* and *Aust-Agder* during wartime. Inland glacial movement millennia ago left the south of Norway with a spectacularly shattered coastline. An aerial view shows the smallest of the islands like clusters of barnacles, a mass of dark centres washed by pure white as the sea roars over them; like barnacles, throughout the German Occupation the rugged promontories shaved the bellies of foreign ships, for the beautiful lagoons and sea fjords hide dangerous underwater rocks. Local schoolchildren accomplished with ease what even the most sophisticated military navigational tool could not: safe passage along the waterways.

Between wars, the larger islands were used by self-sufficient southerners for grazing sheep or cattle. The flocks, sturdy-legged and shaggy-coated, were tended by local herdsmen, who returned to the mainland with their slopping pails only when darkness fell. The milk was rich as the days were long. The names of these islands tell of their former purpose: Calvøya, 'Island of Calves'; Akerøya, 'Island of

Pastures' – *øy* being the Norwegian for island, as distinct from *hølmen*, connoting a smaller body of land adrift.

Småhølmene is not pastoral or pleasant as are its neighbour skerries, where island life flourished once and still today stand monument to its heyday. It must have arisen before Mor-mor like the New World to Christopher Columbus. And if the island once seemed an America, to Mor-mor's great-grandchildren, now needing extra beds to accommodate them, the early settlers made but modest provision. It has barely any grass and what grass there is grows as coarse as matchsticks. There are no trees to break the wind save for a few dwarf rowans, which the wildness of the place keeps from achieving full height. What can Mor-mor have seen about it to captivate? She could not have cared as others did about its obvious shortcoming concerning animal and human habitation, no fresh water on the island, but only perceived what subtle eye and hand might do there to make life bear fruit.

PART I

❖

THE SETTLERS

A letter

I have had a rebirth of memories to talk to you about. My mother's long quiet summers there alone with Lars flying down grandly in his Lobb handmade shoes, with a fillet of beef in his common briefcase and lots of demeaning remarks on how my mother would ruin the expensive flesh! Alone, she lived a life based on the flora and fauna that surrounded her and only used the rowing boat however far she was going — her old leather rucksack full of a mixture of bought provisions and forest chanterelles and blueberries picked on the way to Høvåg. She felt a very close affinity with the eider duck mummies and aunties and was particularly fond of the wagtail parents who dotted about the rocks looking for breakfast crumbs, their little heads nodding as they pattered in swirly circles.

She would have her hair pulled up in a scarf and when dormant in the dawn on her dyne would have all her batterie de beauté lying beside her ready to use once the sun was strong enough to shine on her magnifying mirror to reveal hated wrinkles and imperfections. But to me she was always a beautiful old Red Indian squaw with the seagull's feather in her hair and her teeth very white in contrast to that deep chocolate skin. Better go back to bed and try to sleep a bit before the day begins. I shall write again before I leave for Rode. HAPPINESS I SEND YOU. Mamma

Mor-mor

From what I know of her life pre-island Mor-mor was 'quite a gal'. She had glamour and mystique: dark hair, olive skin, eyes of a curious tortoiseshell. She was a society belle, made conquests, married conventionally. Mor-mor's 1935 honeymoon was a year-long round-the-world cruise, with the likes of 'Bomb' Squires and 'Hendy Old Man', fellow passengers with whom to play deck games between ports. Valuable objects from her travels that I have inherited, and felt in the past should in some way house my grandmother, only disappoint – a golden locket engraved with her name, Olga; a yellow day dress from a Parisian couturier, made for her in the 1930s, which still fits me snugly and manages almost to look modern eighty years on – for it is not things alone that bring one closer to a person. I have learnt not to hold too much to her possessions, to keep Mor-mor under a society yoke. It is Småhølmene that speaks to me of a truer Mor-mor.

Olga Agatha Laura Olsen – Mor-mor – was born on
1 December 1913. She was the only child of Fritz Sigurd Olsen,
of Norwegian shipping stock, and Olga Amelia Ladenburg,
who came from a German family living in London. They
married at Paddington Registry Office on 19 December 1912,
a short distance from their home in Bayswater.

Olga Ladenburg was the first my family knew of bolting women. Almost a year to the day from her marriage, a
daughter was born, also called Olga. Soon after, her
mother took flight and Fritz, mortified by his wife's defec-
tion, set sail for a new life in America, leaving the second
Olga behind. For eighteen months the little girl was shifted
around between her Pappa's relatives 'on appro', tried out
before being returned as a bad fit. She never again saw her
mother, whose death from tuberculosis in 1919 when Olga
was five put an end to all hope of reconciliation. In the end
Fritz's oldest brother Rudolf Olsen and his wife took pity
on the orphan girl, offering her a permanent home and a
new sister, Sofia Helene (Sosse), a child as blonde and
forget-me-not as Mor-mor was gypsy dark. They lived in
an Oslo mansion that today is the residence of the Brazilian
ambassador. Its majestic frontage was drawn back from
the road that follows the fjord's shore along the west of
the city, with views over the yachts and wooden rowing
boats of Bygdøy.

Her childhood if not wholly happy was a privileged
one: shooting parties in the autumn; in winter magnificent
cross-country trips to ski lodges set deep into the forest to

feast on cocoa and sticky cinnamon buns. Summer was best of all seasons. The Olsens left their town house and flew south feeling grateful for the contrast the simple country hut would provide. Here they lived by the sea under wide open skies, remembering all that was elemental and important in contrast to the scenes and noise of the city. The glittering of bonfires and the far-off cries of girls gathering seven types of wild flowers to put under their pillows and wish on at Midsummer's Eve seemed to cast a spell on the land that did not lift until the holidays were over. Nowhere had the turning of the year greater influence on life and activities and the table than in Norway, with its dramatically shifting seasons. It taught the virtue of making hay while the sun shined.

Summer holidays were spent fishing, sailing and swimming, the sport of the day stretching long into evening as the fine weather promised never to break. Nothing material was wanted for Mor-mor to take the best of the world; it was the emotional framework that she had lost out on. There was a trust gap. Her father had chosen not to take her with him to America. It might have been crueller to be kind, for what kind of life could he have offered her there? Had he not remarried and had a daughter by his second wife, a Milwaukeean woman, Olga might have remained under the illusion of his feeling the loss as much as she. No amount of comfort could cushion such a blow. Henceforward Mor-mor would struggle to put faith in, and to keep faith with, those closest to her. Instead she showered affection on

17

animals, household pets and wild creatures alike: the family's two dogs, Ric and Ole, or the Nordfjord horses of the Norwegian *fjell*.

Her falling in love over the summer of 1934, when she was twenty, was surprising as it was welcome. Mor-mor was staying at the house of a friend from Tegneskolen, the Oslo School of Fine Art, on the island of Akerøya. She was drying off on the rocks after a solitary swim when she sniffed pipe smoke on the still evening air and heard the sound of a gramophone belting out American jazz. My grandfather Charles Bennett and his brother, Great Uncle Alfred, were drinking Tom Collinses on the *brygge* when she appeared to investigate, changed coltishly into a dark long-sleeved top with shorts showing off her fine legs.

The Bennett brothers: from their father, Charlie Bennett, an English timber merchant whose business interests demanded extensive travel, they had inherited resoluteness; from their mother, a comely young Norwegian maid from Trondheim, vibrancy. She was admired by the polar explorer Roald Amundsen, who named his Curtiss Oriole plane *Kristine* after her and showered her with presents and dedications. Both Charles and Alfred spoke the classic Norwegian dialect known as Riksmål.

Mor-mor's art school friend, Helle Huitfeldt, was pairing off with Alfred, the elder brother. She was neat, busy and practical, a fine complement to Alfred's sparkle. This meant Charles fell to Mor-mor's lot. He was the sterner brother, yielded less, and again this seemed in complement to Mor-mor's character, which was volatile. Mor-mor awak-ened the playful in Charles, and also some kindly instinct, as a boy will nurse a bird with a broken wing. He was willing to look a fool for one of her laughs as well as to stand silent when her blood was up, avoiding the wrath of the Olsen temper, which eventually blew itself out like the west wind.

Under the northern sun all trace of the steadier, English side of the brothers' temperament receded and they became conquistadors. When Mor-mor appeared, skin salty and eyes bright after her fine swim, Charles determined on winning her. Helle was carefully loading a basket with shells packed with white and brown boiled crab meat and mayon-naise and loaves of dark bread. The rocks were made for picnicking and before nightfall they would go to the seashore to bathe again and eat supper under the moon. She and Mor-mor were to put a seal on their friendship through marriage. By the following spring all was settled: Helle and Mor-mor were engaged women.

The honeymoon took Mor-mor and Beste Pappa – Grandfather – on a world tour. They embarked from Southampton, sailing round the Cape of Good Hope, then stopping at ports from Zanzibar to Colombo and Makassar to Yokohama. Beste Pappa, still besotted, kept a photo-graphic journal of their voyage. Labelling the photographs he repeatedly used his pet name for her, 'Ole', which he favoured above Olga: 'Ole on Way to K's Tombs', and, commonly, 'S [for self] and O'. Even when they returned there was nothing to stop life in London being punctuated by regular trips to Norway. Indeed, when soon after their return the new young Mrs Bennett was ready to give birth to her first daughter, she went back there rather than take the risk with a British hospital.

For two more years island summers went on as usual. Then on 9 April 1940 Germany began its invasion of Norway and Denmark, known as Operation Weserübung. The day previously the fisherman of Akerøya, Axel, had been trawling about four miles from the coast when a submarine under Polish command torpedoed a German merchantman, the *Rio de Janeiro*, in convoy to Bergen with a crew of fifty men and over three hundred soldiers. Her cargo included fuel, ammunition and horses. She foundered and horses and troops were thrown into the freezing water, many perishing from exposure despite the efforts of the Norwegian fishing fleet to save them. One hundred and fifty men were lost. Locals began to describe in lowered voices hauling in pots full of plump crabs with shells the exact colour of the foreign military's uniform. Soldiers' bodies washed ashore in Høvåg and were found there by the young village boys.

It was too close to home. Great Uncle Alfred and Great Aunt Helle fled to Canada while Beste Pappa, by report a man of constitutional seriousness, the sort that takes work and life to heart, conscripted into the British forces. He wore a tailor-made air force uniform, giving him a reputation among fellow officers for being a man of exacting tastes. An army medical revealed unusually low blood pressure, which made him prone to fainting, and the subsequent doctor's report recommended that though as a man on the ground he would be invaluable, he could never think of becoming a fighter pilot. He became a specialist in radar, one of the advances of modern warfare, used to track enemy planes and boats.

Mor-mor spent her war years making impermanent nests with her children, Anne, Christopher and, in 1942, my Mamma, Caroline Elizabeth, a determined middle child. Due in October, her mother was induced a month early so as not to miss an important mess ball. They lived at an RAF base near the Cornish mining village of Portreath, and then, when Beste Pappa was stationed in Middle Wallop, Hampshire, by the famous Box Tunnel. The knack Mor-mor found she had in creating a transportable sense of home was important for her and her children, giving character where they found none. Strongly favouring a warm palette for her interiors – her sitting-room before the war was painted a glossy Chinese yellow – Mor-mor also seemed set on establishing a contrast to the formality she had encountered at her Bygdøy home. Her complexion too suited all that was bold and she wore saffron yellows and alizarin crimsons, with the occasional chocolate brown to bring out the sort of beauty seen in a painting by Velázquez. Nipped-in waists showed off her slenderness of frame that seemed to shake off the spread of child-bearing with enviable ease.

A fourth child, Magda, arrived one year after the daring Allied mission which took the capitulation of the German forces in Norway on 8 May 1945. Beste Pappa was decorated for his daring feats and returned home a hero, to find his wife under some strain. I do not know what Mor-mor's innermost responses to war can have been, what she felt about the realities of the conflict. But those feelings caused by the evacuation of her and her family from her birth country, the country she truly loved, are easier to guess at. That she had a nature exaggeratedly for free movement would have made this even harder to bear. British provincial life was not for Mor-mor. Without her annual visits to Norway, which had of course ceased under occupation, she felt her old life, which had had balance, slipping away from her. She longed to take her children back to her homeland, to the islands, and spoke to them in Norwegian of its stark, rugged beauty like a land in a fairytale. She had few friends among the air force squadron leaders' wives because their small domestic concerns did not interest her and she could not put up a front. She was mystified by the way they mollycoddled their children. British and Norwegian childhood experiences are different without exception. Norwegian children have nature at the back door. With Mor-mor, haunted by her own strange, peripatetic early life, the contrast was intensified. She became neglectful by today's standards of parenting, since following her own inclination always came before the needs of her children, whom she encouraged to run wild.

Mor-mor's selfishness in this respect was in stark contrast to Beste Pappa. He was sensitive and considerate, admiring the strength in and forgiving the weaknesses of others, especially his children. He would not see them hurt or humiliated but knew when to push: he instilled in them the importance of never starting a job without the intention of seeing it through. This made them hold up their heads and square their shoulders. Mor-mor stuck a pin in morale. Feeling dislocated, she made errors of judgement forgivable in themselves, but wounding when they became repeat offences. Her children were caught out in matters of dress: the smocked woollen frock and red shoes rather than the ski suit for Mamma's cameo appearance in the crowd scene in the film *Scott of the Antarctic*; incongruous grey darned school socks and brown lace-up shoes beneath her eldest daughter Anne's national costume when switching on the Norwegian Christmas tree lights in Trafalgar Square. When Mor-mor set her heart on making a necklace of their milk teeth it seemed further in accord with an embarrassing but apparently unconscious tendency she had of singling them out. Wanting only the best, she decreed that the teeth be set at Asprey on New Bond Street – near enough to Beste Pappa's tailor for him to undertake the mission under the pretext of having a new suit made, fielding any censure that might fall his wife's way.

If Beste Pappa had a fault it was his servitude to his lady, giving her ultimate ascendancy. After the war was over, to please Mor-mor he bought a fine half-timbered Elizabethan farmhouse, Chapel Farm, in Buckinghamshire. Another more to his taste was let go willingly.

Beste Pappa drove his large, dark green Bristol car to Great Missenden railway station one morning to catch the train, with Christopher and Mamma in tow. Here was an adventure to give a lift, a day out promising novelty. As the carriages chugged through the countryside they stared out at the smoke clouding the cold morning air, left Amersham behind and went on to Chalfont & Latimer; Rickmansworth palled with a longer stop for the engine to be changed; Pinner, where the Norwegian dentist lived, inspired them as they drew in to the platform to clutch at their jaws in mock agonies; then on past Harrow-on-the-Hill to Marylebone, where Beste Pappa hailed a cab taking them to Asprey.

The London party returned with a box of Fortnum's Elvas plums and found a car parked in the driveway. The house was almost all in darkness but for the study, where the sound of the wireless tuned to a French music station filtered out through an open window. As they trooped up to the door they heard the clink of glasses no doubt filled with Mor-mor's favourite gin and Dubonnet, and smelled the faint whiff of cigarette smoke curling beneath the door. Their arrival had set off a volley of outraged barks from Cheri the poodle, giving fair warning to Mor-mor. It is a credit to her better maternal feeling that she swept up her children in a warm embrace and quite casually introduced them to her caller, whose face was slightly familiar, as 'a distant uncle'. So Mor-mor called the gentlemen who squired her when Beste Pappa was absent.

Mor-mor: she would not have been amiss as a character in one of Nancy Mitford's racier novels, an author whose work she devoured. Like a piece of tracing paper carrying the imprint from the original drawing, she was discovering the impulse to look around her, perhaps even a tendency towards bolting as the first Olga had, allowing her eye to be caught by unworthy men. Terrified she was beginning to act against her principles, against real feeling for her children and husband, Mor-mor sought escape. She planned a two-month-long summer holiday in Norway. Beste Pappa could come and go according to work demands, with Anne, who would be eleven that August, on hand to help with the younger children: Christopher, who was eight; Mamma, five; and Magda one-and-a-half. Mor-mor lost her own concerns in the excitement of bringing them to Norway.

Even the travel was to connect them with a distant past – her past. Mor-mor's father's father, Thomas Fredrik (Fred) Olsen, having spent his early career captaining his father Peter Olsen's fleet of cargo liners, had taken over the business and built a shipping empire, converting the fleet from sail to steam and to purely passenger boats which travelled the globe from the Baltic to the Pacific coast. The family money had a maritime stamp and Fritz, Mor-mor's father, had been a great sailor. Not an iota of family resemblance here, unfortunately. The crossing on the Fred Olsen steam liner that embarked from Harwich was an endurance test and 1947 set the precedent for voyages my family would take over years to come. Before the ship set sail, Mor-mor found her cabin and retired to bed with a bag of liquorice to stave off sickness, while her brood swam against the current of their own nausea until the rough mid-sea when they were washed up and flat unable to move until docking in Kristiansand. Only then did the sweet relief of dry land underfoot and air almost overpowering in its freshness bring colour back into their blanched cheeks.

Mor-mor's heart rose on seeing the southlands again. On first impression it is very different from coastal Britain for there appears to be no tide. This unusual feature is a peculiarity of the Skagerrak, a strait connecting the North Sea with the Baltic. Whereas the British sea coast is exposed to the full ferocity of the Atlantic, the stream there divides through the Channel and up over the northern isles of Scotland, cancelling out much of the impact on reaching Norway. There the tiny inhalations and exhalations of the sea are scarcely discernible to human eyes.

If Mor-mor had a sense of destiny, a presentiment that this was the trip that was to change everything, she kept it under wraps. They were to stay for the summer at a rented house, an old vicarage, in the bustling coastal town of Lillesand. The vicarage had a charming prospect, set back from the marina but commanding a view over it so that it seemed to take life from the regular coming and going of boats, giving pleasure if the afternoon was quiet, or the spirit dull. On the grand main square awash with red geraniums, wagtails fed off biscuit crumbs scattered beneath the outdoor tables of the *Konditori*. This modest shop and bakery was the hub of town life. The year-round inhabitants met daily there to discuss any new scandal over a cup of coffee. Trading ships, tugboats and sailing boats from far afield came and went at the behest of an orderly old harbour-master, ushering in boats from the Blindleia and ensuring there were never traffic jams or accidents.

The Blindleia (pronounced 'Bl-in-lay-a') is a twenty-kilometre inland waterway, running between Kristiansand and Lillesand. The name means Blind Line, and well might it have felt as though you were sailing blind for all the underwater rocks and unexpected shelves, its widening and narrowing passages with turn-offs en route to the open sea. For navigational purposes, the Blindleia is demarcated by white waterside bollards and, when the facing rock becomes too sheer for there to be room for them, bullseyes painted on to the granite. Off-season it is used mainly for trade, but come summer it is a parade water of summer visitors. The double-decker bus-boat, *Øya*, began its inter-port service at the first sign of the impending holiday and all who did not own private boats might take in the scenery from deck: the steeply declining cliffs, the thick woodland and the neat, nestling houses with flags flying. It was a quintessential picture of Norwegian summertime.

The route from Crosshølmen, an outpost of the island of Calvøya, to the Bliksund pier was of particular interest to one of *Øya*'s passengers. The crowded starboard side with its views over a picturesque mainland was avoided by Mor-mor. She looked instead through a pair of binoculars at a small collection of islands lying to the south-east. The sun seemed to shine down upon them so that she wondered in amazement how they appeared to have escaped the notice of the other tourists. Of course she was not the common sightseer. It gave her a sense of déjà vu, of happening on a place once known, or seen in a dream, though it is possible she had never set eyes on them before.

Småhølmene is at its least favourable from the Blindleia. The two outlying arms of rock from the back look like the tusks of a giant walrus. They look preternaturally old and gnarled. Superstition ran high when the fishermen who would go there to set their nets or drop crab pots came back with thick tales of a glow like a will-o'-the-wisp hanging in the Little Beach where the salmon ran.

Mor-mor sailed the *Ole Sørlandet* to Akerøya to discover more from Great Uncle Alfred and Great Aunt Helle, returned from Canada to stay at Shyllevigen for the summer as of old. Standing on a sheltered peninsula of the island, favourable for washing the fishing nets and so earning the place its name – Wash Creek – the house was two-storeyed and painted the colour of Jersey cream. Beyond it, the *Tia Maria*, varnished strakes gleaming, lay at anchor rocking on the gentle currents of the creek. She was clinker-built, handsome and seaworthy. On the tor above the house was a tiny observatory with wonderful views. It had comfortable chairs and provided shelter on a windy day, as well as some insulation for night-time stargazing. Here a round-table discussion took place as to whether Mor-mor could hope to buy Småhølmene. Enthusiasm got the better of them all. In Mor-mor it took stronghold. The owner, a business-minded farmer and landowner, could not think it an asset. Perhaps he would be *relieved* to see it go. She should then give to her children such summers as she had known before the war, with island connections and family ties to give them context.

Already the Norwegian air was proving good for them, and her. As soon as the boat was docked and they were intercepted by their cousins, they could be forgotten about, there being safety in numbers. It was the dream sustaining her through her English exile, which had clapped them all up in chains as she saw it. They scampered over the rocks and glades, stooping to pick wild flowers or to nibble wild sorrel when the beating sun made them hot and parched, for it quenched their thirst. The island was rewarding to the young explorer. The children lost all their shyness, now vital members of a band of outlaws, with Trine and Guri, Alfred and Helle's two daughters, and the fisherman's son, Kay, whose knowledge of the sea was already very great, to bring them out of their shell. The fisherman's hut was on the more exposed side of Akerøya. Nets looped across it like a widow's veil and the *brygge* was piled with faded wooden crab pots. Kay was Axel's apprentice, bringing presents of *torsk*, north Atlantic cod, to Shyllevigen to be prepared according to Norwegian custom: poached in salt water and served with boiled carrots and potatoes. Melted butter and chopped parsley made this a perfect summer feast.

While the children embarked on watery adventures, the talk of the adults took on a philosophical slant. Living through the war had highlighted the important things in life, they agreed. It eroded petty conservatism, perhaps even social morality. The new generation should grow up under the banner of Space, Freedom and Love. Mor-mor was doctrinaire. Action in her had always followed closely on inclination. The small isles should become hers and on them she would build a new civilisation, pioneer a new system, one which disregarded wealth or pomp. The refined existence of ewers and basins at Shyllevigen represented the old values. Summers there had always been tempered by a notion of city, comfort, an outpost of a stifling regime. At Småhølmene she would make wilderness living an art form.

Escaping the herd was important to Mor-mor. Yet, long absent, she was not attuned to the sensitivities awakened by an occupied Norway. In the aftermath of war, bonds between people were closer and suspicion of outsiders at an all-time high. Gossip festered over long cold winters huddled around the kitchen table with a bottle of something warming to help on the debate. Speculation ran rife as to those countrymen who might have aided in the Nazi occupation; suspicion alone earned any Norwegian the name 'Quisling'.

Relations between mainlanders and islanders could anyway be troubled. What did these seasonal migrants, colourful and frivolous as songbirds, know of the harsh realities of Norwegian life? When an Oslo architect arrived at Mor-mor's behest to sketch plans for a *hytte* it seemed to the year-rounders part and parcel of the extravagant tendencies of the blow-ins, whose arrival bumped up shop prices and made boat fuel go through the roof.

A cost might indeed have been spared, for the architect, finding every one of his suggestions quashed with a steely resolve, sensibly swallowed his pride and allowed Mor-mor to direct the building of Småhølmene. His service was only to second her ideas, to become executor of her smallest wish. There was nothing she had not thought of, no subject island-related on which she was without an opinion: she had found her métier at last. Beste Pappa of course let her have her way though it went against all sense. It was not a pearl necklace that she wanted, or silk drawers or expensive perfume. It was his 'Ole' through and through to desire a thing so contrary to 'what women want', and to think her creative vision up to such a magnificent project. It would be good for the children too, for their mother was sure to be happier now she had found a purpose. An island for a mink coat was an extravagance he might allow.

Summer, 1949

With September the Bennetts returned to Chapel Farm. The island was Mor-mor's and there was the promise of a return to it the next spring to tide her over the dreary months. Småhølmene would take two years in total to build. Over that time Mor-mor hopped back and forth, sending the children photographs of the construction with every letter. For them, thoughts of its transformation were distant and exciting. They made ground with their Norwegian despite Mor-mor's many absences thanks to the treasure of a cook, a tall, bony spinster called Dagmar, whose favourite adage went that you never knew how good a thing was until you tried it. Dagmar's housekeeping, dependable and minute, kept home life harmonious. Her firm yet patient habits were a foundation stone.

From her kitchen came the sort of steadying nursery food that holds such nostalgic potential that one yearns for it years later in bed with a cold, or homecoming after long absence. She made classic Norwegian sweets such as *krumkaker*, cone-shaped biscuits filled with whipped cream and *markjordbær*, tiny wild strawberries, and *nougatfromasj*, a delicious praline mousse with nuts so sugary they stuck teeth together as the words twisted on the tongue. Mamma remembers leaving her plate unfinished only once, when Dagmar made ox-blood pancakes, which were wonderfully high in iron and vitamins and utterly inedible.

Chapel Farm was a place to awaken the appetite. In the grounds were trees laden with crab apples for jelly, and walnuts for pickling. There was a greenhouse for growing peaches, figs and tomatoes, best eaten sun-warmed, straight from the vine. Runner beans sunning in the kitchen garden snapped in the mouth with explosions of sugar. Herbs came in profusion, from Florence fennel to Egyptian mint. There were juicy red currants to scatter granulated sugar over before leaving for a few hours to develop a crackling coat. *Rips*, as they are known in Norway, are to be eaten with yoghurt in the morning, or scattered over meringues and cream for a pretty pudding. There was a white mulberry tree. Mamma fed the leaves to silkworms, which, she hoped, would one day produce enough silk for a costume for her favourite doll, Rosemary. She had managed to sneak some semolina from her own bowl into Rosemary's small, pert mouth, which meant that the doll burped unpleasant, old-food smells when she was squeezed too hard thereafter.

There were woodlands of elm, a tennis court and a lake near the big house. Winters came with enough snow that the surrounding land looked like an alpine postcard. The children fastened their skis and skated across the lake. This led to an incident involving the fox terrier, Ole, who fell through thin ice and had to be rescued by Mamma, urged on by Mor-mor, sliding on her belly over the splintering surface to pull the dog to safety. At home she was planted by the hearth where a fire burned cheerfully and told to dry her frock by holding the hem to the blaze. Her legs were soon toasted pink and the terrier curled up on the mat and fell asleep with a toothy grin, snuffling in his sleep. Dogs were given the royal treatment in any household of Mor-mor's and she celebrated her thirty-fifth birthday, in December 1948, holding a canine tea-party, with the standard black poodle at the head of the table with a bib tucked into his collar.

In May 1949 Mor-mor made one last, private inspection of Småhølmene before opening it to visitors. She was in a frame of mind to be pleased with all she saw and determined on enjoying her island solitude. The cabin stood timber-built with a low, curling tiled roof, the vernacular style of the area. It was ox-blood red with white sash windows and doors. It nestled on the spit in the basin of the lagoon, parallel with the mainland. This intimate bay had been instrumental in fortifying Mor-mor's resolve to buy the island. Warmed by the sun climbing in the sky one could dip in and out of the water all morning. Mor-mor was a capital naturist. That spring, the confidence boost of having a lagoon of her own to shield her from any gawping made her naked bathing quite unstoppable. Norwegian law states it is permissible to roam to within fifty metres of a house, even privately owned, setting a premium on Småhølmene's relative seclusion. She plotted ingeniously to scare off the more determined day-trippers by shamelessly displaying her nudity with Cheri as guard dog by her side.

The boathouse was positioned midway up on the right arm of the island. It had two lofty barn rooms: the back area with plenteous shelves and pegging to provide storage space for nets, anchors, pots, spare oars and rowlocks; the fore section sloping away into the lagoon and designed for the overwintering of boats, pulleys and hoists giving it a mechanical feel. Mor-mor trod water at the deep lagoon mouth, where the water turned cold touched by the open ocean, and looked back at the boathouse. It had stable-doors, properly called Dutch doors, and like the main house was a rich red with white piping around doors and windows. It was almost as fine as the main house, and what was better, shielded those living quarters from the view of passing boats.

There were two bridges. Mor-mor ordered that one be constructed across the narrow channel flowing between the spit and the left arm of the island. It stood on stilts with the lagoon running beneath. The other bridge, in a more ornamental style, the Japanese bridge, forded the Little

Bay. This meant free passage over the rocks of the left arm of the island. Mor-mor swam towards it and felt her stomach touch weed, then planted her feet down carefully on to the sand, clouding the water. The Little Bay was the furthest docking station from the bathing steps by the house-end of the lagoon. She waded until she reached knee-deep water then splashed on to the rocks to dry.

Mor-mor roamed Småhølmene choosing names for the sections of peculiar character or distinction. The Blindleia was quiet and the island was in bloom. The rocks of Småhølmene, covered with pink sea thrift from May until August, are prettiest in the spring, when the light is at its most intense. Locals call thrift 'mackerel flowers', for the first flush announces the inland migration of the shoals. The fatty fish made a welcome feast for one, eaten in the last rays of sun while ogled by hungry seagulls. The water settled into velvet at dusk. There was no finer time to be by the sea.

She camped in a downstairs room overlooking *Bitte Småhølmene*, or Tiny Little Islands, where a great black-backed gull pair were at roost. It was convenient to be on the ground floor, connecting her to the outdoors. From the bedroom, two doors opened on to the kitchen and a small washroom. The boast of having en suite facilities, though of the simplest kind, naturally appointed it queen's chamber. The walls were untreated wood, as in all the rest of the house, with the one exception of there being slate around the hearth in the sitting-room in case an ember should catch.

Fire was the great hazard. Småhølmene is not far from the mainland – a mere quarter of a mile – but it can feel so imagining an emergency. The little wooden cabin might burn down in a matter of minutes before rescue came. The romance of having no electricity, the candlelit principle of existence which still governs at Småhølmene, did not diminish the potential threat which naked flames posed. With enough gas canisters on the island to last the summer, this threat was accentuated. To cap it all, Mor-mor was a smoker. She would give dire warning henceforward to family and guests that they act as conscientiously as she herself, stubbing out and disposing of after-dinner cigarettes.

Shortly before midsummer, Beste Pappa and the children prepared to join Mor-mor on the island. Dagmar was to remain at Chapel Farm. She did not think much of the island scheme. It was heathen. Who, if you please, would see to the regular meals, bedtimes and clean clothes? Dagmar's matronly disapproval, and forecasts of a cold spell, though subduing the expression of their excitement, could not extinguish it altogether. For the children longed to see the island again, and even as she stonily packed cases full of the traditional Scandinavian woollen jumpers, *lusekofte* – said to resemble with their signature pockmarks the lice or gnats of the name – they believed firmly the summer would live up to expectations.

Mor-mor had paid homage to an island paradise. She had written letters on thick, Smythson's notepaper describing the magic she saw around her: the eider ducks and how many chicks followed in flotilla; where the gulls had made a nest. Dispatches from another world, thudding on to the doormat at Chapel Farm, they were read by her children at the breakfast table over toast, honey and glasses of creamy milk.

At first their confidence seemed likely to be disappointed. One can never tell what tricks the weather will play at sea, and good sense dictates preparing for the worst. Within days of Beste Pappa and the children's arrival, each one bringing a fresh deluge of rain, the sea had risen over the *brygge* to the stone platform on which the house perched, supposedly safe from winter storms. Mor-mor said they had brought the bad weather with them from England. It was all hands on deck, for such conditions made work. The children's arms began to ache from bailing out the boats. Wet clothes refused to dry. In the sitting-room, the needle of the barometer pointed resolutely to *Regn*, no matter how encouragingly it was tapped; and the hem of the terracotta sofa stuffed with finest goose eiderdown, which Mor-mor had sent over from Maples in London, darkened to a rich peat as the sea flowed into the house. Mor-mor fretted as the pilot light burning below the refrigerator was swept out by a particularly ferocious wave. Added to the chore of bailing the boats, a vigilant watch had to be kept in the kitchen in case of explosion.

High winds and driving rain threatened to overcome reason. Beste Pappa smoked and lost himself in the pages of a novel. All very well for him, but the fug of a Havana cigar made the children sneeze and they grew restless. It was Mor-mor poised to make it the holiday they had hoped for. Never did her spirit soar so as when overcoming adversity. She discovered new occupations to fill long hours when everything practical that needed attention in the cabin had been accomplished. She dreamt up child-friendly kitchen tasks, making *eggedosis*, for instance, which was used to silence whining. The end result was scrumptious, a frothy custard eaten either plain or with pudding berries. The children sheltered under a drippy bit of roof, beating egg yolks and sugar with the old balloon whisk until the concoction turned thick and pale. This took strong arms and lip-pursing concentration. It diverted the sulks on a long, rainy island afternoon.

Mor-mor found another employment for them, helping her to pin postcards on every inch of bare wall in the loo. This transformed it, making it a place to enjoy for its own sake. With the door wide open to the sea, light fell each time somewhere new so that different cards came forward for notice. By pulling the drawstring too, the door swung shut, and in the darkness it became a memory game to think where a favourite image was hung.

The postcards made a rich tapestry depicting the events of a bygone age: the parties of the Huitfeldt family before the war announced with hand-painted invitations depicting ravishing sea-maidens and trident-wielding Poseidons; the fabulous globe-trotting honeymoon, which had opened Mor-mor's eyes to the world. It was a mood board of her likes, illustrating character. She had collected many cards with images of poodles. These were dotted round in profusion: dogs lolling out of the backs of open cars with glamorous-looking women in headscarves, carrying envelopes and roses and diamond bracelets: '*Écrivez-moi quelque chose de gentil à Royan*' and '*De Grenoble, Une fleur! Et un coeur*'.

Such a collection had real family value; like photographs, or letters, it was deeply personal. So when the foreign stamps – which in Mor-mor and the children's view held negligible worth, being the most impersonal element – were somehow discovered by a stamp thief, they were to taste real sorrow. The thief planned his raid for when the family had taken a picnic to Raspberry Island, leaving the house unguarded. He lifted the engine and stealthily rowed ashore. He was very methodical, pinning all the cards back in their proper place though with windows missing. Mor-mor saw the funny side and made the children laugh with his imagined getaway against the current.

When the rain continued, Mor-mor lit the sauna, one thing that was actually better in bad weather than in good. It was an intense experience. The harder the wind blew, the hotter it became, the resin in the wood dripping like hot treacle from the walls and the flames reaching a crescendo of noise inside the burner. A plunge into the ice-cold lagoon felt almost exquisite after ten minutes' cooking. The sauna had a single porthole window facing on to the Blindleia, so that from the top bench, the hottest section, one might watch the eider ducks huddling on wet rocks, or make out the pennant of a passing sailing boat. The cooler lower bench was reserved for small children or those prone to fainting, like Beste Pappa, whose low blood pressure was a bane. For Mor-mor, no temperature was too high, and no volume of steam too dense. She had top-bench pedigree and leapt agilely down to stuff wood into the furnace, or to ladle water with a few drops of pine essence over the coals. Only sometimes did she sit on the bottom rungs practising her Mensendieck exercises, which guaranteed every disciple, frame allowing, the body of a Greek god or goddess.

At last the rocks began to dry and Mor-mor organised what she called a 'topping-out ceremony' for the house. She considered the ritual auspicious, designed to ward off evil spirits lurking in corners, or in the chimney flue that smoked so badly that something malign must be hidden there. Mamma stopped tinkering on her accordion and Christopher put aside his shrimping net as, clutching a heart-shaped garland and Norwegian flag, Mor-mor clambered up a ladder to the roof, where the curling tiles were broken by the swell of a window. This was the upstairs double, which would become the guest bedroom. She attached the decorations to the chimney-top with loops of red-and-blue tartan ribbon. One by one, Beste Pappa, Mamma and Magda climbed after her and edged their way along the roof to pose as Christopher took their photograph.

The children took confidence from the independence that summer allowed. They tracked further on the island, disappearing behind strips of rock to swim at the Velvet Steps, reappearing at Little Beach where the water was so shallow you could reach in and lift hermit crabs from the sand. There were always new gullies to explore, or even just new ways of getting to the same place. It was a compact island, a half an hour jogging point-to-point, once proficient footwork got them over the difficult sections. Their legs were soon scratched and bruised with trials and races, but such minor battle scars went unnoticed in the bliss of unconfined wandering. Granite and lichen toughened the soles of their feet so that they almost forgot to mind about stepping on the broken shells of water snails dropped by a seagull's beak. They discovered play areas as well as contrivances for pleasing Mor-mor, who appreciated shows of initiative: a fishing expedition returning with six plump cod gutted and beheaded while out at sea, or collecting mussels.

For this they had designed a clever though uncouth method. They climbed the length of the right-hand arm of the island, carrying buckets and a long broom, to a cleft in the rock where sizeable mussels grew. Fresh salt water washed over the black shells welded to the tumbling reaches of granite; in stormy weather the sea dashed so fiercely over them that it earned the place the nickname Cornwall. Magda, who was three-and-a-half, pointed to a good thick cluster and stood out of harm's way, while Mamma edged lower to where she could reach for the mussels. Then she jammed the head of the broom down and held it for a minute quite still. The mussels, opening to feed, fastened to the bristles so that each time the broom was hoisted back six or seven came too. Back at the house they cleaned the shells over the *brygge* with a scouring brush. They counted between them how many mussels they might each have at supper as a way to forget the calluses developing on their hands. When all were gone over they left a bucket outside the kitchen door for Mor-mor. She steamed the mussels in a covered pot with a little chopped onion, cream, white wine or vermouth if there was any, and cut thick slices of bread to mop up the juices.

All island harvests were best prepared without much adornment, from the very fresh fish and shellfish to wild leaves and berries. Mor-mor was an expert in simple preparation, possessed of the instinctive frugality and good sense of the forager. She hunted for chanterelles, boletuses and creamy white puffballs on mainland pilgrimages to meadow and forest, where she wove between the mysterious tall anthills carrying a chipped china bowl for the booty. Mamma trotted behind her clutching a little basket of her own to fill with mushrooms, and learnt to identify the safe varieties. Back at the island, the pair would sit out of the wind in what Mor-mor called 'sun stripes' – strips of light filtered through windowpanes on to the floor – carefully extracting the pine needles and dabs of earth from the gills to burn in a sauna so that it smelled of the woods and trees.

Mor-mor cared about food and would go to some lengths to find or catch the best of it. In the summer, her cooking was at its most inventive, for scarcity bred imagination and limited resources, skill. Nothing on the island table was ever without some marvel attached to its preparation: the jam Mor-mor had made with island raspberries to sandwich with whipped cream in a *sukkerkake*; the cordial pressed from the tiny wild blueberries that grew above the boathouse, by the juniper, which was used to infuse *viltsaus*, a melting sauce for ptarmigan or willow grouse with *geitost* cheese and cream. Island food, you see, had a particular nostalgia and placidity about it.

Sometimes Mor-mor pushed her foraging instincts too far. A jungle of angelica bushes with their edible leaves demanded fancier work. The bakery cakes were strewn with sugared angelica and Mor-mor did not see why she should not give the home-made version a go. The plants on the island were covered in furry, bright green caterpillars that left tiny bite marks, like a pincushion, so you had to hunt around carefully to find the unblemished leaves for crystallising. The care did not stop there, for it was easy to forget a pan of boiling sugar when the outside called, and Mor-mor, vague and impulsive, drawn to swim or lingering too long over a cigarette, burnt many pans irrecoverably.

When the sunny days brought out in her a terrific indolence, and she gave in at last to the tiredness that is known after a great work is completed, her character seemed to waver and shrink. In its fulfilment her *raison*

d'être had been cruelly deprived her. She had trans-
mitted to her children throughout the island project
skill, creativity, enterprise and best of all imagination.
The island was theirs for the taking. Their daydreaming
made of seaweed, silk cloth; of oyster shells, ancient
pyramids; of abandoned eider duck nests, treasure troves.
Mamma and Magda picked soft down from among the dead
leaves and dry heather for Anne to make blankets and
pillows for dolls. These raids took place shortly after dawn,
when they crept furtively over a naked sleeping Mor-mor,
lying on her *dyne* waiting for the sun. Beside her was her
foil crescent and North Sea water for reflecting the sun
when browning under her chin. A magnifying mirror
was set out to inspect every imperfection in the harsh
natural light. Beste Pappa registered anxiously the signs
of ennui.

The children dared each other to snatch one of the
sweet butter buns from the bread tin. *Bøller* came plain,
or studded with raisins, with chocolate chip ones saved
for special occasions. The crust was deliciously yielding,
the tops of the buns glazed with egg and milk so that they
baked to a tawny gold. Flecks of spice ran through the
crumb, the tiny black dusting of ground cardamom seed.
If Mor-mor found a depleted stock when she opened the
bread tin she'd let out a yell, and an angry, *Drittunge!* –
Dratted child! Breakfast took place late in the morning
by which time they were always ravenous. A snack was
worth quite some risk.

When the children returned from their games Mor-mor got up reluctantly, removed to the shade of the kitchen and began to set out the breakfast things. She put water on to boil eggs and set out the salt cellar and the pepper pot; generous seasoning elevated a soft-boiled egg uncommonly. Norwegian hens' eggs are particular for having shells that are uniformly white. Mor-mor saw this as a canvas of possibility. When done, she scooped the eggs from the water and painted the shells with cows and sheep, or drew eyes and mouths to make funny faces.

She cut even slices from a loaf of dark bread, carefully remembering to rub the blade with oil before she began – rye bread could be very sticky. From the store cupboard came jams and honeycomb. There was fresh milk and butter collected from the dairy in Lillesand, as well as the rich cheese made with twice-boiled goat's milk. On buttered *knekkebrød*, which was slightly sour and deliciously crunchy, providing much-needed contrast in taste and texture, *geitost* was no longer cloying. It was wholesome breakfast food. The children ate with their legs dangling over the *brygge* while Mor-mor and Beste Pappa leaned against the house, cracking the shells from their eggs and piling the shards into the bottoms of their eggcups.

The only exception to the form was on a birthday – Anne's birthday was in the second half of August – when breakfast was carried rattling on a tray to Mor-mor and Beste Pappa's downstairs bedroom. The four children were allowed to pile into the bed, scattering crumbs as they devoured special celebration pastries. These were called *kringle*. Plaited, or shaped into a figure-of-eight, they contained raisins, citrus peel and nuts, with sugar nibs creating a snow shower effect.

Everyday breakfasts, so long as it was not too wet, only ever took place outside, on what Mor-mor was moved to name *Kongeveien*, or the King's Road, after she had found a discarded street sign in the outskirts of Oslo and taken it home with her. Now it was nailed by the sauna, announcing a flight of stone steps: the breakfast steps. These led up to the wooden bridge connecting the main spit to the left arm of the island. Here, the children ate with a fine view out to Seagull Island and beyond, where their gaze fixed on the lonely lighthouse far out at sea. This was an exposed existence that was delightful to imagine, secure in the knowledge of a home on dry land. The sound of the morning chorus drifted across the lagoon.

The birds of Seagull Island were hostile to intruders who moored their boats for a picnic, drawn by the place's apparent desertion. They sounded an alarm better than any guard dog and were treated with respect by Mor-mor. She looked after them in her fashion. At her cry – *Måke-måke-måke* – herring gulls, great black-backed gulls, lesser black-backed gulls, flocked to her, knowing it meant a feed. They were wild things and would not land until she had removed to a distance. So it was that very little was ever thrown away, being given either to the birds or the crabs, which crept out from under weed when a fish was being gutted on the *brygge* or scrolls of potato peel were scraped from a board.

When grocery supplies needed replenishing, Mor-mor would row to the mainland to a provision bunkhouse run by the dour Mr Thorsen and his wife. A deep distrust of the mechanical meant anything was better than using an engine, and so shop visits depended on clement weather. When the wind was against the boat it took sheer brawn to make the crossing, the distance of half a kilometre, and then the prospect of a brisk quarter-of-an-hour walk from the jetty at Bliksund. Thorsen's was set deep among the twists and turns of Høvåg. On solitary trips, Mor-mor returned carrying little bunches of wild pink clover, sea campion, violets and forest harebells. She made hand-kerchief bundles of forest mushrooms, or woodland berries to be spiked with cocktail sticks and eaten as refreshers after a heavy meal.

An expedition to buy provisions, with its promise of an ice cream, was tempting to the children. But, trotting after Mor-mor clad only in a scanty brassière top, with an elk-skin rucksack ready to fill with rations on her shoulders, the children found these trips mortifying. The vinegar-faced man who lived by the postboxes, where Mor-mor posted her Smythsons, made no attempt to conceal his disapproval of her devil-may-care attitude to town standards. Girls peeped out from behind netted windows and admired her pleasing, shapely figure and the way Mor-mor tied back her hair in a bright French silk scarf.

The road inland met Kassen Tassen the Troll, who lived beneath a bridge brandishing his nasty-looking club at the boats that went by. Peering over the railings it was only possible to see a villainous peaked cap poking up from the rock, and the blunt top of the troll's bludgeon. The work of a sculptor, Kassen Tassen was brought to life by folklore. It was said the troll demanded that those wishing for safe passage under or across his bridge answer a riddle. Failing this, they must give other forms of payment: gold coins, a first-born child, even their life. Norway was a land steeped in mythology and Mor-mor was well-versed from youth. Tall Norwegian pines cast shadows over the winding roads of Høvåg, engulfing her figure as she strode on ahead, falling into piebald patches of light and shade. So dense were those forests that, looking hard at their outline from the island, Mamma thought they resembled the troll's gnarled face and beard.

When rainclouds again darkened the sky, August was at an end. Mor-mor was beginning to hunt down lost socks and jumpers to take back to Buckinghamshire for the British winter. Strong currents from the south swept through the lagoon. Jellyfish collected below the *brygge* and around the bathing steps, where they spawned soupy clouds. Before the rain came in earnest, an army of black slugs appeared on the rocks and around the butcher's block on the lagoon-side used for the washing-up of plates and dishes.

It was a coin's toss between seeing the last days out with what was in the store cupboard, or going to the mainland for victuals. Not fancying the trip herself, Mor-mor looked around her for a suitable emissary. Beste Pappa had returned ahead of the rest of the family to England and work. Christopher was not a strong rower and hated rain. Magda was too young. Anne had been staying overnight with her teenage cousin at Akerøya. In the end, Mamma was sent alone, the rollers tossing her light rowing boat about mercilessly. It was a fortnight from her seventh birthday and her last ounce of strength was sapped by the voyage. She was completely traumatised, and angry with her mother, under whose instruction she had set out.

Mamma

Mamma, with her round face and good appetite, was the apple of her nurse's eye: 'The pick of the bunch,' Dagmar said. 'Line' had a middle child's hunger for attention as well as for food, always hovering by her side, taking crumbs from the batches of cakes and biscuits that were made freshly through the week. When the day's work was over and Dagmar sat down heavily in her rocking chair with a cup of hot coffee, Mamma climbed on to her lap, pressing her cheek to the old woman's and listening to the noisy sucking as Dagmar filtered every sip through a sugar lump nestled in her cheek.

While Småhølmene had given her a taste of freedom, Chapel Farm, and the characters that belonged to it, provided her with security. She befriended the gardener, George Warner, who gave her freshly cut bunches of snapdragons for the kitchen table and lettuce for the family tortoise, Theseus. Dagmar and George were locked in stealth combat over the kitchen garden. Though the gardener left baskets of all the well-grown marrows and horned parsnips outside the kitchen for Dagmar's use, she stole out to pillage the younger, sweeter morsels for the family.

Dagmar's springtime meal of lightly poached young vegetables – she called it 'a vegetable cabaret' – was an annual celebration. It included tiny beetroots, fennel, asparagus spears, peppery radishes, lightly stewed artichoke hearts and onions no bigger than coins. Generous bowls of mayonnaise, made from eggs with good bright yolks and light oil so as not to overpower the flavour, were provided for dipping, flecked with sprigs of curly parsley. At Chapel Farm breakfasts, lunches and teas, and the cordials that accompanied them, owed much to the woods and fields around the farm.

Mamma was drawn to George and Dagmar because they were simple, steadfast and loving. They anchored the seasons of her year. Sensing softness, Mor-mor determined on transferring Mamma to agricultural school to steel her edges. This educational background and the savageries that would occasionally interrupt the peace at Småhølmene – the scream of the gulls in the middle of the night when a mink was going for their eggs; learning to gut a fish – would add to her prevailing sensitivity a strange imperviousness to the grislier aspects of nature. She could never see an animal suffer without thinking of putting an end to its suffering, and was happy henceforth to help in the ritual beheading of the Christmas goose.

At Småhølmene summers came and went, experience gradually layering on itself to fix habit and traditions. Ordinary days followed ordinary patterns, with the example always set by Mor-mor. While her island ways went absolute and unchallenged, Beste Pappa was losing his grip on authority. He struggled to overcome the idiosyncrasies of the cabin, which were better understood by Mor-mor and the children with every season that passed: how doors slammed if too many were left open at once, making the house a wind tunnel; how the sitting-room might have to be evacuated when a sauna was lit as smoke billowed out of the shared flue running through the foundations. Though the children helped him, instinct could not be taught, and this was where Beste Pappa fell short.

Get-togethers played as big a part as ever, with boats rocketing between the islands of Akerøya, Calvøya and Trondarøya to issue summons: blood was thicker than water and family ties still held sway. There were casual lunches of *smørbrød* with eggs and fish roe, curd cheese, smoked fish and pickles, followed by fruit picked from an obliging branch or raspberry cane; lavish cocktail parties with martini and champagne, spilling over into princely suppers of wild salmon and crab.

Long winters make of most Norwegians fine merry-makers come summer. They are inclined towards hospitality, always willing to help a neighbour in need. Growing wealth was also making its mark, breaking down social barriers and transforming island life. Islanders' children received good educations and left to find jobs in the cities. Summer was more than ever a time to hark back, to raise a glass to a world that could never be recaptured. Great Uncle Alfred and Great Aunt Helle were true countrymen in this respect. They were sociable and generous, bastions of the summer life of islands. This made them naturally popular. Mor-mor on the other hand was not widely liked. She had to be prised from Småhølmene and seldom returned an invitation. Her antisocial tendencies were singular and inexplicable.

Of all the seasonal highlights, it was Great Uncle Alfred's birthday, on the seventh of August, that promised most. The parties at Akerøya were legendary. When a couple of days before the event an invitation was made in person by Great Aunt Helle, appearing in the lagoon in *Tia Maria* and hollering to Mor-mor, the latter felt annoyance that her morning peace had been shattered. When Axel, extending his round hauling in the nets, arrived with a jovial wave to ask, 'Will I be seeing you there?' she challenged him in the full glory of her womanhood, wanting to confirm ETA. He clapped a hand over his eyes and refused to speak to her until she put on a robe.

Alfred's birthday celebrations took place either behind the house, where there was a sheltered garden, or, if the evening was still, on the *brygge* at Shyllevigen where Beste Pappa had first set eyes on Mor-mor. Experience had taught otherwise than to trust first passions. Great Uncle Alfred, who was a confirmed topper-upper of glasses and only very reluctantly gave to teetotallers the cherry pop substitute for real drink, put a match to Beste Pappa's nostalgia with his refills. Great Aunt Helle's wonderfully bright full-length tunic swam before his eyes as she passed round dried meat and sausage. Supper came as a welcome sponge: lobster mayonnaise or fresh white crab meat with lemon served on triangles of buttered bread, followed by chicken and then *Napoleonkake*, the fantastic cream cake that came from the bakery in Lillesand. The children put on theatricals, or a musical review, as after-supper entertainment, before escaping to their games while the revelry went on.

Alfred could be found on mornings after, swaying slightly in a mist of Captain Morgan spiced Jamaican rum as he raised the flag at sunrise, a patriotic ritual unthinkable to waive even when still tipsy in the dawn.

The Bennett clan was soon to chasm. The divorce of Mor-mor's adoptive sister Sosse and Henrik Huitfeldt, Helle's brother, had a domino effect. Unrest swept through the family and the country, as the government's *samnorsk* policy to standardise Norwegian encountered fierce opposition. The big house at Calvøya, Calvehagen, became home to Anita, Henrik's second wife from Switzerland, and her son Peter, providing a step-cousin for Mamma and her siblings. Sosse and her new partner, the Norwegian actor Knut Wigert, became active members of the Riksmål Society, campaigning to preserve the traditional written language in Norway. Other exponents were Henrik Ibsen, as well as the authors Gabriel Scott and Knut Hamsun.

Sosse published a series of tracts under the title *Fri Sprawg*, or 'Free Language'. Still today the language comes in two established forms: Bokmål, 'Book Language', based on the Danish; and Nynorsk, with its roots in original Norwegian dialects.

Trouble was brewing between Beste Pappa and Mor-mor, brought on by the admiring men who visited Chapel Farm when he was absent. Winters were the danger time, for husband and for wife. At Småhølmene, Mor-mor was beyond reach of temptation, but not in England. Uncertain what it was she ran from, uncertain what it was that she looked for, it was a trial by error. To this the children were witness and judge. There was the assiduous Hooky, for instance, whose long snout it was terribly easy to caricature, to make longer and knobbier and more absurd. Such calf love could not sustain: a relationship needed a sting to keep her. Hooky was eclipsed in Mor-mor's affection by Lars Farnes, an agent for a camera and film company and a man of social ambition and expensive tastes. He hid the stumps where he had lost several toes in a wooding accident in pricey handmade loafers. His handsomeness was of the strong and lean-bodied, Norwegian sort, with sandy hair that was going grey around the ears. He appealed to the part of Mor-mor that had ambitions to something greater than happiness, which could only be realised in equal partnership. She had island thoughts when she looked at him.

When things finally fell apart – Mor-mor dispatched a Smythson with the falsely gay announcement, 'Daddy and

I are getting a divorce!' – Beste Pappa retreated into the world of Chapel Farm, blocking out Mor-mor. He had been a man of the wrong mettle for his wife; there was something too diluted, too accepting in his determining on blindness to Mor-mor's *affaires*. Now his pride was worn, and his patience at an end. He towered in resolution. He secured Dagmar's services as family cook indefinitely. She had seen it coming and with her 'business as usual' attitude contained the damage.

Beste Pappa was not vengeful, but vengeance fell to his hands, for the children, to a man, sided with him and Chapel Farm. When has self-interest in a parent ever warmed a child's feeling towards them? Children need some cotton wool, the feeling of being put first. Mor-mor had embarked on a personal journey, one they could not follow.

She bought a house to overwinter in Holmenkollen, near the ski jump, and where come spring a great lake within walking distance offered opportunities to bathe, enough to satisfy even her. Holmenkollen is on the outskirts of the Norwegian capital. The comfort Mor-mor took from being back in the Oslo of her childhood was much needed. In the 1950s divorced women were either painted as victims, or reviled. Publicly held as *monstre sacré*, Mor-mor found sympathy lacking. Meanwhile the children of divorced parents faced either contempt, or pity. Mamma became woundingly known as 'Double D': the only girl in her agricultural school with both a *dyne* (rather than a duvet) and a divorce.

Wanting a chance to commiserate, Mor-mor travelled to England to Chapel Farm. Finding a downstairs window open, she stole in and hid herself in the old priest's hiding place on the second floor. When the children returned, she leapt out and pleaded with them to move back with her to Norway, which caused alarm and had the opposite to the desired effect. Of the four, only Mamma was willing to spend the holiday in Norway, and Beste Pappa pushed that she spent it at Akerøya as the ward of her uncle and aunt.

Mor-mor's divorce from Beste Pappa and subsequent remarriage to Lars Farnes was the cause of a cooling-off in her friendship with Great Aunt Helle, whose loyalties were divided. Great Uncle Alfred of course *could* only side with his younger brother, and she must stand with him. Meanwhile, at Småhølmene, harder for Mor-mor than the loss of her friends was the affection that sprang up between her middle daughter and Helle. Helle was a woman who could be relied upon for good sense and steady morals; she had backbone, without which either is defunct – she held the family together. Here was a real role model. Mamma took to calling her aunt *Beste Venninder*, supplanting Mor-mor's former position as Helle's best friend. And when Mor-mor arrived at Shyllevigen it was Helle's protection – standing mightily on the *brygge*, the wig that she wore to cover thinning hair slightly askew in her anxiety – which safeguarded the happiness of the niece by sending her mother away.

Mor-mor learnt to loathe interference from the outside world during the summer of the great divide. The seagull feather worn in her hair made her an island Hiawatha. She let the dog climb up into her and Lars's bed with the bus driver's summons, *Ta plass!* – Take your seats! – and they slept three in a bed, which was quite a cram on the narrow Småhølmene cribs. (Mor-mor bought a pillow embroidered: 'Your dog loves you when nobody else does.')

Four years passed without any lessening of the *froideur* between Mor-mor and her children. Anne, Christopher and Magda stayed away. Mamma continued to 'holiday camp' at Akerøya with her cousins, building up quite a large acquaintance among islanders. She crept into her teens dreaming of exciting trysts with one of the more handsome fellows of the Sørlandet, who were competently rugged, yet shy, so that things remained very innocent. When a large gang of them went to Kristiansand intent on finding a nightclub, they were at once so genuinely exhausted with the journey – which took over three hours along the Blindleia in the stately *Tia Maria* – and so dismantled by nerves to be in each other's company, they simply sat on the jetty where they had docked the boat for an hour, before turning around and going straight home again.

❖

With Great Aunt Helle standing in over the summer, and Anne through the winter, there was just about enough care for Mamma to feel mothered. Anne's 'coming out' for the debutante season in 1958 deprived her and the others of an authority figure. Mamma was sixteen at the time and in need of someone to look up to. Dagmar was stalwart as ever but what did a confirmed spinster know of coming-of-age concerns? Mamma stood to gain everything from building bridges with Mor-mor and encouraged the others to follow suit. A fifth summer brought about reconciliation. She, Christopher and Magda reunited with their mother on the islands.

Småhølmene was just the same. Mor-mor seemed just the same. And because they were changed themselves, they relished continuity the more. Many of the old traditions were still fixed practices, from breakfast on the steps and saunas on wet days, to swimming from the Velvet Steps whenever the weather was fine enough and collecting mussels with a long broom at Cornwall. Only when the heat sat on the water like a mist with not a breath of wind astir was time idled away. On such days, they sat leafing through the glossy magazine *Ballyhoo* and struggling with the broadsheet bulk of *Aftenposten*, saved from the last visit to Thorsen's shop, or might simply recline on the steps of the house to squint into the sun.

Lars was only present at weekends, business keeping him in Oslo through the week. His arrival upset the balance at Småhølmene. It appointed two days out of the seven special, for to civilise was his intention. And what a battle he faced.

He carried the best fillets of beef with him from Oslo in his leather briefcase. The quaint stock of kitchen tools having made him recoil, a meat tenderiser, heavy griddle pan and bamboo-handled steak knives that the meat should be given proper treatment, cooking and serving followed soon after. Leaving these to soak overnight, Mamma found the handles had split and the knives had to be thrown away.

Lars was an epicure who relished his supper. Meals took ages with him around. It had become a competition among Mamma, Christopher and Magda to be the one to escape the table to wash up. This was one of the island's more painstaking processes, nursing the theory espoused by Mor-mor that food tasted better when a pan had not been cleaned too thoroughly – when a built-up encrustation, with its accompanying flavour, like a cassoulet pot's, came from each cooking vessel being given what amounted to a deglazing. To hands cold from sitting idle, the warm soapy bucket of water brought feeling and colour back into fingers; to a mind fatigued with attention, the sound of voices from the back drifted across the house in a soothing murmur: the lagoon was at its most tranquil at dusk when birds settling on the water spread dainty rings and the seaweed made popping noises beneath the *brygge*. Mamma was forced instead to watch gull feeding time, Lars cackling over the attempts of the male gull to bolt a well-picked T-bone.

To please him Mor-mor cooked grand meals with French butter sauces in place of the usual, simple, sea-sourced feasts. One exception was her *fiskesuppe*, which still evokes the very best of summers on the island. It suggests bounty, as do the similar fish soups of the south of France, but is a triumph of making-do, relying for success on the ingenuity of the cook and her knowledge of local produce.

Magda and Mamma worked together to drop the nets at dusk the day before the preparations were to begin. Sorting the fish worth eating from those best made into stock also fell to their lot. Mor-mor liked to infuse extravagant amounts of saffron in the broth – not as unauthentic as might be imagined, for the sailors of the Norwegian Merchant Navy brought back with them spices from Europe and beyond. Mussels were gathered and scrubbed over the *brygge* by Christopher. He peeled the potatoes too, which were then put aside in a pot of fresh water to stay white. The aromatic soup with its chunks of island fish may have pulled the party together but Mor-mor always headed operations.

She was that rare thing: a totally natural cook. Island cooking could stand up to no less. Having no shops to tide you over in an emergency taught the art of substitution – recipes simply could not be followed to the letter. Mor-mor kept few cookbooks at Småhølmene, and those she had were written on in the margins like anything. Mamma too learnt to be a great annotator of recipe books, with irreverence or criticism even in the notes about the need for extra sugar or more flour; or a valuable friend paid tribute to in the scrawled essentials for a crunchy crumble topping that would do for apples, quinces or rhubarb.

Monotony was a danger. But monotony was inevit-. able! Even for the most ardent cod-lover, by the third day it tasted tediously plain, and one longed to be in the position of the dinner guest in the old joke, offered a choice of cod or salmon and replying, 'You cannot serve both God and Mammon.' So you taught yourself to enjoy its cheeks and brain, even the tongue; fried or smoked cod liver, which was delicious on bread; you poached it, fried it, baked it, turned it into patties; you flaked it into a pie or set it over smouldering beech and juniper branches to cure, turning the fine white flesh translucent like exquisite marble. So prepared it was excellent in a salad with olives, waxy potatoes with skins still on, capers, parsley and lemon, and of course lots of freshly ground black pepper.

Butter and rapeseed oil were the fats used in cooking, food of the land, ineradicably part of the country's topography and climate. The Scandinavian kitchen had remained largely uninfluenced by the tastes of southern Europe. Rye and spelt flours were used as commonly as wheaten in breads and flatbreads. Potatoes were eaten year round, with special celebrations for the new potatoes that arrived at midsummer; vegetables were mainly roots and anything that could survive, or was bettered by, extreme cold. This meant cruciferous vegetables such as cabbages and sprouts, underground vegetables like Jerusalem artichokes, beetroot, carrots and scorzonera. Horseradish thrived, ideal for grating into soured cream, a condiment so strong it could make your eyes water. Perishable supplies were kept fresh under a trapdoor in the island kitchen.

Health-giving vitamins and minerals more often came bottled, for it was in the preserving of ingredients that Nordic food really excelled, from salt barrel to vinegar jar. Pickled cabbages and beets, dill-cured salmon and lingonberry conserve were all benefits of a climate requiring hibernating tendencies. Knowing how and when to harvest was innate, and how best to use a surplus. Any fish that Mor-mor did not need the day it was caught was wrapped in pages of the *Aftenposten* and left in the fridge to be made into *fiskebøller*, or fish balls, highly seasoned fish patties using up spare or inferior fish. Every town had its own recipe but the best came from Risør, where recipe quantities were a fiercely guarded local secret. For special occasions, *fiskekaker* could be made, superior to *bøller*, covered in a rich white sauce with capers, butter, cream and parsley. But in general such extravagance was frowned on in island cooking. There was nothing like a cold, spare winter to teach you the virtues of foresight. It was said Norwegian girls married only when they had nine different biscuit recipes by heart, but they also came to the altar with a sharpened frugality and a gift for economy and good housekeeping.

Things tasted different in the summer and usually much better, especially when they came after exercise and fresh air. The island of Justøya lay just within kayaking range of Småhølmene. Its central attraction was Brekkestø, with its pretty whitewashed houses and bustle. Crews from tall ships sailing in from Sweden and Finland to replenish fuel supplies demanded the attention of an idling youth in shorts, who sat bronzing himself beside the single fuel pump. Ice cream bought at the kiosk was best enjoyed people-watching. But first the trouble of choosing flavours, for the catalogue was bewilderingly long. The best fruit ice creams were of course made with wild forest berries when they could be picked and stirred in whole, or puréed into the custard base. The subsequent freezing process seemed to intensify the flavour and lessen the impact of the sugar, making them very refreshing. But it was the traditional *krokaan* ice cream that was Mamma's favourite. *Krokaan* is made by pounding caramelised almonds. With its slight crunch, like butterscotch, the powder can be blended into a vanilla cream to great effect. *Krokaan* can also be eaten on its own or used to decorate cakes.

Mamma ate her two-scoop cone swinging her legs over the *brygge*, playing her feet against the nose of the boat as it rose and fell with the waves and looking despondently at her scratched lower legs. She had been so unfortunate as to inherit from her father's side of the family the infamous 'Bennett ankles', which were no ankles at all. She had also grown into a rare antique loveliness, with high cheekbones, very clear skin that turned to honey when it saw the sun, and dark brown eyes.

Mor-mor had vanity, but not enough to spoil her appreciation of beauty in others. She noticed Mamma had

65

become a beautiful young woman and longed to polish her beauty hard – to make it perfect and impregnable.

Life on an island is a breath away from captivity. Mor-mor, in love with the captor, had a taut, complex relationship with the place, and escaping from her sometimes tyrannical infatuation was necessary to avoid arguments. Being away from Småhølmene brought Mamma interludes of peace whether an excursion was dreamt up for fishing, collecting berries or boating. It also gave her the sense of a victory won for she, too, was falling under the island's spell. Mamma found solace in the rocks and the birds, which became friends as year in, year out they nested on the same old promontories of Cornwall, Bitte Småhølmene and the cap of Bringebærhølmen. A favourite spot of hers lay at the far reaches of the left arm of the island, where, gazing out at Calvøya and its remote outer isles, and Seagull Island with its brackens and lichens, hours went by unnoticed. The water was deep and inky and the sky was at its biggest, absorbed by the sea where the horizon met in a fine line. The Far Rock was a place to feel a little lonely, but sometimes, when a guest was staying, it had to be shared. Thus when a friend of Lars's was weekending at Småhølmene, a rare instance of an outsider being invited to the island, Mamma and Mor-mor, both competent fisherwomen, planned an afternoon outing there with the intention of spinning a line for cod.

Mor-mor called this method of rock-fishing *kaste sluken*, or cast-spinning. Among the family it continues today, seldom with much confidence in the outcome. Drop-line fishing, which is also practised, involves little skill but much patience and it is more reliable in its provision of supper. To do this, Høvåg locals go to sea early in the morning, or at dusk, often in pairs. It is really a two-man job, one holding the boat in position as the other dangles the line, standing up when the sea is flat enough for added thrust. The more eccentric Småhølmene method, like fly fishing, is each man for himself. The wind plays havoc with the line, and it is all too prone to catching on weed or rocky crevices when reeling-in. Competitive frisson comes from every catch being recorded and historicised as a victory won.

When Mor-mor had demonstrated how to swing the hook with enough line so that, on the up throw, the weight of the spinner meant it flew out some distance, she handed the reel to Lars's friend. She retreated to a safe distance from the firing line – a sensible precaution even if the thrower was experienced. When the friend let go of the line awkwardly, on a backwards shot, both Mor-mor and Mamma instinctively ducked and covered their heads. They heard a yell and looked up to see the unlucky guest clasping her ear, a thin trickle of blood emerging between the fingers of her hand. Mamma fled back to the house and returned panting, carrying scissors and a roll of bandage. She gouged the hook from the lobe as Mor-mor covered her eyes and turned pale.

Mor-mor's civility did not outlast the holiday. Her charm had a sliding scale. Weeks in close company sapped

her energy. Long summers at Småhølmene were worse than
Christmas for eruptions of family tension. Such unreliable
guardianship left Mamma, Christopher and Magda feeling
as though they were treading on eggshells. Lars tired of his
wife's temper and became inattentive. August dragged.
With the inevitable end-of-season departures came a
mingling of sorrow and relief. September was a time for
Mor-mor to recalibrate. She stayed on the island alone,
which for her was a tonic. The autumn air, abundant cold-
water fish and the first of the game birds, which Mor-mor
crunched her way through bones and all, made it a favourite
season. True it was melancholy to be alone. But knowing
that, by October, she would have returned to the Norwegian
capital helped her to make the most of her woodland walks
and naked swimming.

The Old Order

A large modern townhouse of early Georgian design, 40 Chelsea Square was the well-appointed London home of Great Uncle Alfred and Great Aunt Helle. It was to wintertime what Shyllevigen, their island home, was to summer: a comfortable, civilised hub, where an open-house policy ensured a steady stream of guests. Bennett family Christmases had always been, would always be, held here. As is customary in Norway, celebrations took place on 24 December, not the twenty-fifth, which was a rest day.

Dagmar took centre stage over the build-up at Chapel Farm. She welcomed the Bennett children home for the holidays with her comfortable uprightness and the delicious smells emanating from her kitchen: a hit of ginger from baking *peppernøtter*, and the whiff of candied fruit from the warm Christmas tea bread, *Julekake*. The weeks of Advent passed in a blur of snowy walks, tea and decoration-making. They wove heart-shaped paper baskets in two colours for the lower branches of the tree and stuck edible tails into sugar mice to peep from the opening. They studded orange peel with cloves to burn in the fire for wonderful smells on a rimy evening.

Mamma's thoughts through all this travelled north. She minded very much what she saw as her mother's exile. It almost spoilt her enjoyment of festivities, appealing to her inner worrier. Christmas turned the sights to Christian redemption, to forgiveness and charity. She had to remind herself that Mor-mor had made a choice, and that the pride that stopped her from reaching out might be offended by shows of pity. The festive season was bad for Mor-mor. Her inspiration was gradually blunted kowtowing to Lars's demands. He mined into her savings with endless unnecessary extravagances of apparel, and by picking only the choicest food for the Yule table. What was the good when it was only the two of them to enjoy it? Mor-mor did not want Beste Pappa but missed the family life that he represented, and never more so than at Christmas. She threw herself into dog worship, dreamt of the islands and, vicariously, of her children.

On the twenty-fourth, the whole Chapel Farm entourage rattled up to London in the family's Bristol car. Beste Pappa hauled out presents as the girls smoothed down their national costumes, waiting for the yapping of Great Aunt Helle's pack of dogs to subside as footsteps approached the front door. The shrill Yorkshire terriers all had black bows in their fringes, like those of colonial wigs, and they had to be waded through or one risked being engulfed in the siege.

The buttery-mustard smell of roasting chipolatas – Helle's favourite – drifted along the hall from the kitchen.

No one was allowed to see the tree until just before present-opening, to gild with anticipation the impression it made in the dim sitting-room, candles in the branches of pine and a cache of presents glittering beneath. At three o'clock *riʒcrem* was served, a luxurious rice pudding lightened with beaten egg white, with a blanched almond hidden inside, the discovery of which decided who was to open the first present. Mamma, who always had second helpings whether or not the almond had been found, poured a moat of cream around her bowl and sprinkled cinnamon and brown sugar on top. Great Aunt Helle merrily speared cocktail sausages, holding a little ivy-pattern napkin in her fingertips. Great Uncle Alfred, set aglow by a tumbler of rum, tapped his toucan's beak of a nose with a finger and proposed a toast. Whenever someone said '*Skål!*' the adults locked their eyes and drained their glasses, as though daring one another not to blink. Embarrassed by such displays, Mamma played with the dogs, pulling their ears and making snuffling noises. If her mother had been there, she would have caught her eye and smothered a laugh.

Dagmar remarked that the feast that was to follow required one to have saved some appetite. She was too God-fearing to extol gluttony for its own sake. There was spinach soup seasoned with nutmeg, with buttered egg boats floating on the green sea. The soup was Dagmar's speciality and she always ensured each egg boat had its own individual scattering of parsley to help digestion. Aquavit was then served with gravlax, boiled potatoes and a special thick sauce made with fresh dill. This was unutterably delicious, spiced with Dijon mustard, sugar and vinegar; pungent and uplifting, all at the same time. Roast goose wrapped with bacon came with such a variety of potatoes, vegetables, sauces and jellies that every inch of sideboard was taken up with plate or tureen. Then came pudding at last: the humble 'peasant girl' of stewed apple with crispy sugared breadcrumbs, and her 'wedding veil' – lightly whipped cream for spooning over the fruit. After the feast was over, the cousins linked hands around the Christmas tree, singing '*Så går vi rundt om*' – 'Then we go around'. The chorus is very long, and after all the heavy food it was a dizzying exercise.

The larder bulged for the window days before New Year. The stairwell gave telltale creaks after midnight, when Beste Pappa sneaked down to pinch bacon-wrapped prunes and rice pudding from the larder. Some things tasted better eaten clandestinely. Dagmar tut-tutted disapprovingly and said Mr Bennett ate more in his dressing-gown than he did at mealtimes proper.

✺

In spring 1962, Mamma prepared to embark for Australia, to work as a governess in the outback. She bought the £10 migrant ticket to Queensland with her own money, for in going she went expressly against the wishes of Beste Pappa, who wanted her to do the season in London. The motives for her departure were scarcely decipherable. There was a great deal of romanticism behind the plan; that much was certain. Mamma had a long-distance crush on the dashing Australian Lew Hoad, a legend in men's singles tennis. Daydreams of meeting the great man certainly held sway, for the boat would stop at Sydney, where she had promising introductions and might snatch an encounter. There was also rebelliousness to her actions. Mamma, though sensitive and easily hurt, was a strong character and, in a contained way, unconventional. As surface calm might tempt the fool-hardy swimmer into a strong underwater tow, so Mamma's docility concealed currents unexpected and even danger-ous; dangerous because they pulled against the mainstream. Beste Pappa was keen to dam this if he could.

Anne was to be married to a handsome bachelor, and bridesmaid's duties were among the last of Mamma's engagements before departure in late March. Debutante life was not for her. She was too shy to enjoy the parties and was sure to be found in the kitchen talking to the mother of the hostess. Rebellion would give her courage to enjoy the fruits of adventure. On the twenty-eight-day voyage, she won a fancy dress competition for her cavewoman costume and became mascot of a gang of emigrant Yorkshire miners. She arrived at the start of Australian autumn. The scenery from the railcar in which she journeyed onwards was breathtaking, if stark. She was met by pony trap at a deserted station. Only then did the magnitude of her task, and the loneliness she would face, become apparent.

Eleven months later, Mamma returned to England clutching a volume of Banjo Paterson's poetry, a present from her employer. It had been an entirely new kind of education. Freedom improved her both in spirits and confidence. When she had arrived in Sydney for a polo tournament, she was besieged by admirers who, knowing her ancestry, competed to be the one to take her to see Henrik Ibsen's *Peer Gynt* (eventually she went three times in one week). An island sojourn was needed and she embarked for Noway to give herself breathing space. Mor-mor had a friend staying and spent longer than ever over *Kongeveien* breakfasts while listening to a new transistor radio, the hard-boiled eggs to mash over buttered bread kept warm in a dividable china chicken on the top step.

After a brief period working in London, Mamma became engaged. It was not original. It was a return to the old order. Simon Barrow was handsome and confident and a good match in temperament, bringing out her more gregarious side. They married at Holy Trinity Brompton in June 1964. Though not impervious to the charms of the Norwegian archipelago, he was every inch an Englishman. Aged twenty-three, Mamma had my half-brother, Thomas, and then three daughters followed. The diluted Norwegian blood that ran through them was given vent and strengthened at Småhølmene, as Mor-mor introduced her grandchildren to island life. There were second cousins at Akerøya to play with, building on the good relations between the two islands. The children were made aware of the privilege of being descended from the original island settlers. They inherited friends and enemies on the mainland, and some of the elders' superstitions and proclivities found ways into their natures, penetrating like the wind.

Any past misdemeanours of Mor-mor's were forgiven and forgotten. Perhaps it was that Beste Pappa's second marriage to a Norwegian war widow squared things for her children. This union took place in November 1969, when Thomas was four and Sasha (Mamma was reading a great deal of Russian literature through her pregnancy) just over a year. With a mother's knowledge and insight she could see that, though Chapel Farm was good for them, island life, Mor-mor's invention of the world, the reason she had flown, was better.

Likenesses are known to skip a generation, and though relations were at times strained between Mor-mor and Mamma, the grandchildren were both admiring and submissive. Much that had been difficult for Mor-mor's own children to live with, her impetuosity for instance, and mischief, were positive attractions to them. When they arrived at Småhølmene, thrilling presents awaited them, from sugar-coated jelly-men or Fox's lemon chews under their pillows, to battery-powered torches. She gave them besides a romantic vocabulary. Instead of the dull, scientific word 'phosphorescence', Mor-mor called the lights that twinkled in the sea after dark 'the mermaid's pearls', so making cleaning one's teeth over the *brygge* really magical. Naked swimmers were 'Raphael's angels'. She taught them to notice the things in the foreground – the cotton grass, the caterpillars on the angelica bushes, the down left in birds' nests, the patches of sorrel and thrift – the island's small, secret pleasures. The long perspectives, the expansive surrounding of sea, sky and rock, impacted without need of introduction. These things stirred the appetite, made sleep fuller of dreams and gave length and substance to a day.

Whatever activities were dreamt up, Mor-mor was always expedition leader. Grandchildren swam around the island with Mor-mor in the vanguard disregarding stinging jellyfish and tickly weed, or made deck hands on her long fitness expeditions in the rowing boat. When she moored to explore and forage in faraway creeks, tossing the boat-rope over a boulder and wading through the shallows to reach shore, they leapt out after her, clutching baskets to fill with wild provisions. Striding confidently through the forests with her elk-skin knapsack on her back, Mor-mor would stop at a clutch of chanterelles among the pine cones, smelling sweet like apricots.

The chanterelle is the star of woodland mushrooms, superior to the common boletus, or cep. Mor-mor would oversee their cooking for, though a simple enough process, the devil was in the detail. No salt could be added until the mushrooms began to brown, nor had one to risk stewing them so that they lost all their fine flavour. Such a feast was not to be let down by poor presentation. Mor-mor kept an immaculate table. My middle half-sister, Emmeline, who liked supermarket salad cream to the point of being unable to eat anything without it, was flatly refused the plastic bottle at table, though she got round this by hiding it on her lap.

Years could not smooth away all Mor-mor's rough edges. Lars's death, in the summer of 1977, came as the first shock. Mamma and the family were at Småhølmene when they received an explosive Smythson from Oslo. The envelope lay in the green tin postbox at Høvåg, in the section reserved for the islanders' correspondence. Mamma, expecting news of her youngest daughter, who being too small not to be a nuisance had been left at home for the holidays, opened it immediately. Mor-mor's handwriting quavered with emotion. The message read: LARS IS DEAD. That evening at Småhølmene, two swans flew low over the lagoon, catching the attention of Mamma who was busying herself with the washing-up. Swans were not native to the island, and she took this for a visitation by departing spirits.

With Lars gone, Mor-mor was keen to sever ties with Oslo. She determined on selling the house in Holmenkollen, anticipating sanctuary in London. All her children had homes of their own and operated an open-house policy. Thus when she met an affable but hard-up young man in need of a place to stay, Mor-mor felt she could afford to be magnanimous and lent him the place. Only after a long, trying winter, she regretted her decision. But it was then too late for retraction. The beneficiary was discovered to be a worthless scrounger, intent on holding Mor-mor to their verbal agreement handing over the rights to the Oslo property. A court case took place, which left Mor-mor homeless.

Dependence made her fractious, history repeating itself. She took the contraceptive pill, saying it 'made her feel young'. She dyed her hair and plucked her whiskers. Only her skin betrayed her age, the bargain she made with her sun worship. Years of exposure had crumpled, like old leather, cheeks that had once been smooth, and plump. North Sea water was still her friend. While staying at Mamma's house in Kensington, she was spied by the postman reclining topless in the first-floor window, wearing the silver foil crescent tied round her neck to brown her under-chin.

At Aunt Anne's London house, there was still more chicanery. Anne's eldest daughter, Sibella, was a great favourite of Mor-mor's, with her insouciant, stylish way with dress and charming, clever face. And Sibella was proving to be artistic, which was delightful to Mor-mor, since it was a trait that came straight from her. She would disappoint Sibella's suitors by answering the telephone to tell them in her crotchety voice that her granddaughter was out, regardless of her actual whereabouts.

Mor-mor was alone when she died, Anne's family having left their house in the country for the races straight after breakfast. She set out into the park at her usual brisk pace wearing a borrowed red mackintosh for the unsettled Easter weather. Then she altered her gait as though she was practising taking big steps. The farm hand who discovered her was the last person to be deceived that she was a much younger woman than she actually was. Mor-mor would have been thrilled at the report he made of finding quite a young lady collapsed in the woods.

PART II

GRANDCHILDREN

Mamma's diary entry, 26 August 1974

Embarked from Harwich on the F. Olsen ferry with Simon, Thomas, Sasha and Emmeline, plus lots of luggage and food. Usual argument over the bunk beds and a windy crossing with Thomas being sick and Sasha only too hearty, asking for endless food and wanting to dash about and explore. I was helpless and pale and sat stoically on deck, wrapped in a rug wondering why it is that, remembering how ill I feel each year, I don't fly instead. Drove from Kristiansand in sparkling sunshine and arrived at Bliksund to find a flustered Antonson and Inge, who had expected us for the last four days and sat up and waited for us on stormy Monday night. Mrs A. had her dressing-gown ready, so as not to be caught in her nightdress like last year.

Filled Dagmar with all the stuff and chugged out to Småholmene — still the same thrill as we rounded the corner into the lagoon with the boats neatly moored and the stable doors. Some kind person has given us one new red rowing boat, Line 11, for Thomas. Mor-mor left presents for the children: soap, tooth-mugs, corn-on-the-cob picks, tea set and a Fred Olsen tie for Thomas. Went off to explore the rock pool and noticed a lot of plastic waste all around the coast; determined to clear it up and not throw such stuff into the sea myself.

Child of the Island

I was the last of a second wave of grandchildren, and too young to have one memory of Mor-mor to call my own. Instead, recollections were hand-me-downs, like clothes, coming from older siblings, or cousins. The Mor-mor chronicles were bedtime story material, as well as the fallback of family get-togethers. Never was a company so animated as when recalling Olga's peccadilloes. These were tales that invited dramatisation. I was charmed by what was eccentric and awed by what was formidable in the renditions I heard. I trembled under her temper, which was legendary – 'the Olsen temper' that still flashes up from time to time in one or other of her descendants. The idea that Mor-mor possessed almost as many dark shades to her character as she had flashes of brilliant light, made her in my eyes more heroic in scale. Though there was much to disapprove of, there was plenty to captivate, and to inspire.

In Oscar Wilde's essay 'The Decay of Lying', a case is put forward for 'delightful fiction in the form of fact', and the appeal of artistic representation over real experience;

I certainly allowed myself to create from the stories a picture more perfect than true. This swagger portrait Mor-mor was something I treasured, having almost as much to do with myself, the artist, as it did her, the muse.

Northern summers brought me tangibly closer to Mor-mor. While I missed out on the hands-on initiation elder grandchildren had enjoyed, she became known to me through her greatest achievement: as the late discoverer and founder of Småhølmene, my childhood island. Here, her laws and dictates prevailed. Objects littered the cabin as though at any moment she might pick up, say, the carpet beater hanging in the room known still as 'Mor-mor's', and begin whacking one of the dusty floor-mats with it. I arranged the shelf of age-whitened seashells beneath her actual portrait, which hangs in the living-room, with a sense of maintaining the shrine. The watercolour was done by a guest, who framed and sent it to Mor-mor by way of a thank-you present. It shows her naked back view, arms raised in enigmatic salute. Seabirds flock overhead, dazzling white against the blue sky. Year in, year out, I looked at this painting. It took life as my experience gave the scene context. I was becoming spirit-bound to Småhølmene, just as she had been before me.

※

One of my earliest Småhølmene memories is watching Mamma, like a woman from a Norse saga, rowing me over the waves around the island. Her arms had the same varnished mahogany look as the timber boat, a pine skiff, which came from the Hardanger province: a skiff long and curving, resembling the famous Hardanger fiddles hailing from the same region. The sound that the joinery made was musical too, like the A-note tuning an orchestra, eliciting an answering humdrum of birdcall from Seagull Island. Sailing on the open water the movement was graceful, even sultry, as if the boat became a part of the natural movement of the sea. I reclined back to rest my head against the keel rib, enjoying the heavy pull of the oars, which made Mamma frown with the effort, and the ripple of the water beneath us that implied no effort had been made. She, like Mor-mor, rowed for exercise, and would have ventured further had the boat not begun taking on water, like a thirsty man, so that she was forced to stop and float while she bailed out. The lifted boards revealed a viridian green undercarriage swilling with seawater. The emptying sloshes disturbed a heron, which took wing and was swallowed by the gentle curves of Raspberry Island.

In the still I hung over the sides of the boat, dipping my fingers in the water, spying passing jellyfish far below. The outline of their stinging trains appeared much longer so deep underwater, fading like an aeroplane trail into the blue. I counted a tally of Canada geese and oystercatchers, eider ducks and the small wren-like birds that nest in tiny crannies of rocks. Then we set off again. Mamma became absorbed by the rhythm of rowing and gazed, not at anything in particular, but at the general flow of the wash behind us.

❊

The next most pressing memories are invariably those of my early island birthdays, or Great Uncle Alfred's celebrations, which went alongside. I was born during a violent storm in London on 6 August 1981. Mamma emerged from the bathroom naked at eight-and-a-half months pregnant to be met by a friend of Thomas's creeping up the stairs, returning from a night on the tiles. I gave a huge somersault and thereafter arrived in such a hurry Pappa missed the delivery, at St Mary's in Paddington. Great Uncle Alfred was seventy-four the following day. Festivities went on at Shyllevigen as party-goers toasted the new arrival, who, according to Mor-mor's arsenic, the lottery of birth dealt a cruel blow in making a girl.

For the next two years I was left behind when the family went to Småholmene for the summer. I stayed in Cheshire with a quiet, elderly couple whose own children had flown the nest long ago. This same couple had taken on, from Mamma's first marriage to Simon Barrow: Thomas, only boy; Sasha, eldest girl; Emmeline, middle girl; and Rebecca, youngest girl. From Mamma's second marriage to my father, Mark Culme-Seymour, in December 1978, there was only my elder full sister, Georgina, or 'Dordie', and me. From two I was of island age and began to feel the advantage of an August birthday.

There was something about a Norwegian birthday. The days were only ever sunny, and the evenings balmy. The birthday cake – the *bløtkake* (pronounced 'blurt-kak-ir') – was very grand. It somehow tasted just as it sounded, stupendously rich. It squelched jam, cream and nuts, and its thin layer of marzipan covering stuck to the roof of the mouth with every bite. It was the quintessential summer cake. I knew the advance planning it took to get and this only heightened the pleasure. The cake had to be ordered from the bakery in Lillesand a week or so before. On that trip, to which I was accessory, all knowledge of the *bløtkake*, and the birthday, was denied by Pappa, who did the ordering. The next trip, the pick-up, I was left behind at Småhølmene. It seemed an act of God whether it arrived in one piece or not, and, to help things on, I prayed silently for a smooth crossing for my father back from town so the cake would not be bumped about on the waves.

At teatime, when it made the centrepiece of the table, I like to believe every one of my siblings was as pleased to see the thing as I was, since it was a general favourite among us. But it had my name written on it in chocolate piping – the Norwegian spelling, with an 'h', Mathilde – and I was quick to claim the decorative marzipan pink rose.

My birthday teas at Småhølmene were but a warm-up to Great Uncle Alfred's fantastic night-time revels at Shyllevigen, eating *kreps*, tasty saltwater crayfish, and, for all the adults, drinking strong spirits. The way Mamma plied the company at Småhølmene with hydrating weak tea

and lemon, and pressed on guests dainty cucumber sandwiches, highlighted some anxiety about the coming
debauch. It was the same crowd at both parties: the Akerøya
cousins; old Axel, the Akerøya fisherman, and his son Kay;
the Calvøya cousins Peter Widmer and his boys; then us.

❈

Norwegians are great appreciators of family. When numbers
swelled after Mamma and Pappa united clans – Pappa had
two children from his first marriage, who sometimes joined
for summers on the island – we became the boast of the
Sørlandet. A Norwegian lifestyle magazine, *Hytteliv*, with a
leader describing Småhølmene as 'The Pearl of the Ocean',
featured a photograph of us arranged in height order on the
brygge, Pappa looking heroic at one end, me in a red Helly
Hansen life jacket at the other, pulling what Mamma called
'the little-mush face'.

In London, where the family base was, the very thing
Norwegians were wont to celebrate – our marvellous
number – was an encumbrance. We stuck out among the 2.4
families in the neighbourhood and children hate to be different. A uniformed 'Princess Christian' nanny was hired by
Pappa on a live-in basis to look after Dord and me because
he felt Mamma was spread too thinly. Veronica was not like
the redoubtable Dagmar, Mamma's nurse, being neither
aloof nor aged, neither stern nor Scandinavian. To our
delight we discovered that the island had the same effect on

her as it had on all of us, peeling her like an onion to reveal her inner layers of being. As we rid ourselves gratefully of smocked dresses and shiny buckle shoes, our town regimentals, so Vron emerged from her drab beige uniform a wonderfully colourful creature. A number of wacky things about her came to light at Småhølmene, such as her belief that she had access to the spirit world. There she won over the younger of my half-sisters, whom she embarrassed at home, interpreting every unexplained creak or thud in the cabin as a ghostly mariner rising from a sea grave.

Pappa's investment in an extra pair of hands was well worth it. He was often away, a true product of the hard-working, hard-living 1980s. It was cocoa that made him tick and made him rich. He travelled in pursuit of the finest beans to Ghana, Venezuela and São Tomé. Meanwhile Mamma and Veronica held the fort at home.

'Home' was a big townhouse on a one-way street in Kensington. It had floors and bedrooms enough to accommodate us, though not so many as to prevent Mamma recurrently dreaming of opening the fridge to find an extra room inside. Mamma was always a fantastic dreamer. Sometimes we were woken by smothered screams – she slept with a pillow over her head – or, passing her door, which she always left ajar, overheard uneasy mutterings in Norwegian. Over breakfast, Mamma would explain calmly that she had been having 'a Småhølmene dream': that the island was being ambushed, or the hut was burning down.

It is not surprising that she had an active subconscious or that Norway frequently penetrated through. The average 'school day' demanded military precision. With a sixteen-year age gap between eldest and youngest child, there was always someone who needed taking somewhere. In a barracks existence, Mamma was field marshal. Even during the holidays she was on duty. The Christmas and spring breaks were spent making improving visits to museums; taking brisk exercise in Royal Parks; kitting out the troops for the restarting of school terms. Island living exploded on her year bringing the relief of monsoon rain after long drought. It soothed, uplifted, restored. Freed from the worry of constantly watching her offspring, she got on with her own thing, except to notice that we were getting what Mor-mor would describe as *melkesjokolade* and that the sun was streaking our hair with auburn.

Dordie

Born on the Sabbath, Dordie was a fair, bonny baby and a good sleeper. She was Mamma's fourth girl and her conception had been a miracle. Mamma had had one of the first pioneering reverse sterilisation operations in the capable hands of George Pinker, royal gynaecologist and obstetrician. Telegrams and letters of congratulation flooded in from England and Norway when Georgina, named after the celebrated doctor, was 'fished out' on St Swithin's Day in July 1979. She was the perfect extenuation of my parents' marriage and the upheaval it had caused.

Two years later I came along all too easily and with a knack for troublemaking. I refused to sleep, which caused great strain. Mamma grew gaunt and pale from tiredness. My half-siblings stepped in. There was always a sister ready to whip me away when Dordie needed attending to. Indeed, when Mamma was discharged from the hospital after having me, it was Emmie who cradled me importantly for a photograph in her yellow OshKosh dungarees and candy-pink shirt, while Mamma held Dordie by the hand. 'The little ones' was established status for us, one that nothing could or would ever remove.

No sooner had things settled in the nursery than my older siblings competed to oversee our bath-times and bedtimes, which must have been extremely handy for Mamma, as well as creating constant noise and good humour, stimulating for any household. They jostled to steer the pushchair and once Thomas most unfortunately tipped me out on to the street. Though half-brother and -sisters, they loved us like whole and were, from the start, intensely involved in our upbringing. So great was their influence over us, there was risk of its inciting future rebellion. Yet, shamed by their laughter – more effective than any parental discipline – we became eager to correct bad behaviour. We wished to be like them, and so we listened and obeyed when they spoke. The three older sisters in particular operated as a unit. Their voices sounded as one, a funny, bullying and loving confederacy of sisters, Dordie and I a breathless audience.

❖

Dordie's founding experiences at Småhølmene in 1982 were typically those of any young islander, as were my own when I followed on a year later. She stooped to fill a bag with mussel and snail shells, almost upsetting her balance on the rocks, for it was an island that needed two hands to navigate.

She swung on the stable-doors of the hut wearing a fringed sombrero hat, swimming costume and water-wings, or was trussed in oilskin trousers and clip braces to accompany a wet fishing expedition. Red admiral butterflies visited that summer and settled on her arm without her trying to kill or bottle them. She ate *bøller* at the summit of Videheia, had a cut knee plastered and kissed at the boat after a stumble in the forest, and was fussily checked over for ticks when she was again at Småhølmene. Though everything in the sail-loft was much too big for her – flippers, snorkel and mask – she stood decked out anyway and looked on while the older girls powered up and down the lagoon blowing out spray like whales. While their preparations were under way for a midnight crabbing expedition, Dord watched miserably knowing she would be left behind.

For the next two years, my first and second on the island, everything seemed to be stamped with a Fred Olsen logo: the table mats and prints of early passenger ships, hanging on the wall in the sitting-room; the caps pulled over our heads in the midday sun; the decks of cards Dordie and I used for games of Snap!

Småhølmene continued to be reached by us the hard way, a method involving endless driving and long, painful boat journeys on the Fred Olsen fleet, which I learnt to dread, having inherited Mor-mor's incurable motion sickness. Dordie had the constitution of a sailor, as did Sasha. Pappa also had sea-legs. His captaincy positively encouraged marauding behaviour, and the run of the ship was theirs while the rest of us stewed in our uncomfortable cabin beds. On one crossing, Dord took her first solo flight, lifting off deck into the storm while Pappa and Sash grasped a hand each. She was rewarded with a *Daim-is* and stuck the chocolatey wrapper into her scrapbook together with a coaster ringed with dark brown circles from Pappa's coffee cup. One way or another it always took us a day or two to recover from the trauma of the rough delivery.

Getting to Småhølmene, we went through an acclimatisation process. We kicked off our shoes and felt rock beneath our feet. We visited the postcard loo for its fantastic views and museum quality. The cards were faded and peeling. We pulled the chain and pumped the valve until the cistern refilled with a whoosh of fresh seawater. We raced to Mor-mor's room to choose *lusekofte* knits from the cupboard, starting our conversion into islanders. Soon I had a favourite *kofte*, a present from great-grandmother Kristine, nicknamed Kiss, to Mamma, which was cream-coloured with pale blue arrows and stars in a horizontal pattern. The cardigan had brass buttons decorated with what looked like the outline of the flower of the wild strawberry plant, with tiny bracteoles and sepals alternating with each petal.

The first night's bedding-down had a clean-sheeted luxury. Further into the holiday, speckles of saffron-coloured lichen and sand from the Little Beach – where, because it was shallow, the water stayed almost constantly warm, inviting paddling – found a way into the cotton, not helped by our dragging *dyner* out for lying on in daytime. Tired by fresh air and activity, we slept deeply anyway, anti-princesses oblivious of the 'pea' mattress-leagues under.

Mornings brought revival. Our batteries fully recharged, Dord and I ping-ponged around the rocks. 'Home-style' games of the sort we had at our disposal in London did not come until two or three weeks in – my birthday – by which point we could do well without. We never admitted this to Mamma, who continued to persuade us to leave toys behind in London with the promise of what was to come on the sixth. The only time I ever remember Dord in a temper was when I unwrapped my birthday presents with deliberate slowness, knowing she was as eager as I was for what was inside. She slammed her fist hard on the table, upsetting the birthday breakfast.

Småhølmene had a Midas touch. Everyday experience turned to gold on the island's shores. Mamma's written commentary in family photograph albums conveyed this. 'Dordie and Tilly in the Småhølmene Grass' was packed with meaning: our complete satisfaction with nothing else besides ourselves and a game of being marooned. The Velvet Steps was a second Eden, with tropical grasses and water plants. The sandy Little Beach seemed permanently rippled by a soft wind, and the rocks lushly green with yellow-green moss. Trips to Lillesand to buy provisions were a tale of top engine-speed and *soft-is* ice creams. Like all good adventures, these voyages ended in a feast: salty pink prawns bought at the quayside fish market, mayonnaise squeezed from what looked like a toothpaste tube and something we called Dead Man's Leg, a white bread loaf that looked alarmingly like a prosthetic limb. We caught tiny shrimps and starfish, lying on our stomachs prodding nets into the popping weed beneath the *brygge*. When we caught a pugnacious blue crab, Dordie scribbled a sign that read: 'Bewear [*sic*] of fingers! SID FISHES' (she meant the punk-rock musician, Sid Vicious), and left it over the bucket weighted by a stone.

❊

Being the latecomers in a large family was not without consequences for Dord and me. Småhølmene showed these up starkly. Summers there became a metaphor for the constraints and freedoms our family position would give us in life. How we yearned really to 'own' the experience of an island summer apart from the interpretation of our siblings. There was very little to be discovered or imposed on a place so rich and categorical in its family history. Wanting to be pioneers, we found ourselves part of a ready-made system. We felt in danger that nothing we made of Småhølmene would ever surprise Mamma, who could refer both mischief and triumph to something she and her sisters, or our own older brother and sisters, had done before us. We longed to impress her by some discovery, to earn her praise for a show of unusual pluck or derring-do. Landmark achievements, like single-handedly landing a fish for supper, or swimming the length of the lagoon for the first time, were not stand-out. She encouraged Dordie and me to name an area of the island, a place of our own choosing, but our names never rang as true as the Velvet Steps or Little Bay, Little Beach or Cornwall: names that had Mor-mor's clearance.

Salvation came from an unexpected source. Released from many of the worries that spook a first-time parent, Pappa nudged Mamma into giving us a long leash. This drove Dord and me to break ground. Otherwise Mamma's boundless understanding and sympathy – we were her cherished babies – might have smothered.

Dord and I took possession of Småhølmene, discovering early we had a natural aptitude for the place. I became adept in the complex choreography of the rocks, for instance, miraculously always balanced and upright, while having two left feet at home. We always went barefoot. Even when I stubbed a toe and cried, Mamma dried my tears, declaring I had become an islander, for no summer was complete without its quota. It was experience of a different sphere. The island was an extension of home, but better, because of the lessening of interference, both paren-tal and sibling. We built our own private worlds there around the rock pools and cubbyholes so well suited to our size. We were like sponges, soaking up the necessary skills. With water all around, learning how to row was most pressing. So Dordie and I set ourselves afloat.

❈

We could soon be left alone in our walnut shell and not worried about by anybody, bobbing safely on the lagoon. The boat for young novices had once been handsome fire-engine red, but was now faded poppy. *Little Thomas* had seen over a decade of summers at Småhølmene and was in used condition. Her hull was scratched from being dragged over barnacles to shore for picnics on Elephant Island. These were worthy battle scars, as I saw them. I longed to be the boat's master and commander. I urged Dordie to build up stamina in lengths up and down the lagoon, from the bathing steps to Little Bay and back. The round trip was almost two hundred metres. We perfected lightning turns, careering back and forth.

If the lagoon-mouth created a natural boundary to these sallies, the gull channel was a hinterland before the sea proper. The stream running through it was partially protected, Seagull Island acting as a dam to the worst of the swell. But the currents were unpredictable and navigating them presented a real challenge. Like choosing and preparing the picnic for ourselves – rye bread pockets, Jarlsberg or a cold fishcake, puddings of chocolate and oranges – it was a marker of independence. When first we nosed out into this stream, it felt like being propelled forward by rapids. *Little Thomas* breezed through the faster water like a kite in high wind, the oars escaping from their rowlocks with our every attempt at control. The only way forward was with courage, to relax and let feeling take over.

On the promontory on the far right of the island, looking on to the mouth of the lagoon, there nested a pair of great black-backed gulls. They let out rocking cries before dive-bombing smaller boats with keen eyes flashing. And *Little Thomas* was no match for wild sea swans, fairly common since the time of Lars's death, and so much more vicious than the gulls. Feeding off underwater grubs, their upended tail feathers looked to me like the sails of model boats. Watching a gaggle of hungry swans was as good as a Sunday regatta. We were warned from getting too close by an Akerøya cousin, who had once had to defend himself with an oar after a territorial cob cornered him on an island peninsula. Swan attack was a frightening thought. Dordie might be lookout while I rowed, or we switched roles.

We were very close, reading each other almost like extensions of our own consciousnesses. There was only the most moderate competition between us; rather we complemented each other, a double act. It helped that the constraints we felt as runts of the litter applied to us both, so that any cap or limit became a joint disappointment, to be shared and so lightened. In my imagination, I had been cast adrift from the rest of my siblings, with Dordie my lone companion. I guarded her jealously. Any perceived change of allegiance was a treasonable offence as I saw it. Though Dord had her insurrections, they were small and carefully contained. One night she pencilled a note that she slipped to Mamma across the supper table, which read: 'To Mamma, Can I stay up for a bit? Love, D.'

I was aware that the two years that separated us meant something, but I did not think it was enough to matter.

When it came to it, it was not, certainly not enough to divide us as friends. She never complained at the endless rounds of the childish board game 'Jumble Sale'; tirelessly 'farmed' snails (dividing snails by their shell markings and moving them accordingly between rock pools); and put up with stories at bedtime that she had heard many times before, such as my beloved *Jim and the Beanstalk*, written and illustrated by Raymond Briggs. We were both addicted to dressing up, bucking the histories of the clothes inherited from our elder sisters in plots of our own make-believe. Two threadbare strawberry nighties we wore led to games of strawberry-picking before bed. Often I became so carried away I would bite Dordie hard on an arm or a leg. Our stripy sundresses came from the Finnish company Marimekko. We had the same bowl haircut ('Too Short Hair!' Mamma wrote in her diary after an attack with the kitchen scissors) that made us look rather more like little boys than little girls, with our scraped knees and rougher, tougher island propensities.

Dyne Mornings

U p a steep flight of steps, across the landing from the upstairs double, is the dorm. There is scarcely any natural light, for the one small, south-facing window is obscured by rock. There are always night lights on the bedside table, and torches for when it is extra dark. It has four box beds, narrow like in a sleeper compartment on a train, with drawers beneath for clothes. The sloping rafters have built-in wall-paintings, as the resin in the wood makes mysterious shapes that, like clouds, morph when looked at a long time. It is a cosy, quaint room, slightly different from the rest of the house. This is where Dordie and I slept.

Lying in our strawberry nightdresses, our teeth tasting salty from brushes rinsed in seawater, we drifted into the deep, dream-heavy sleep of the sea – 'negative ions,' Sasha said – hearing dismayed groans from the sitting-room as our sisters lost games of cards, or backgammon. Once all were gone to bed, the hut began to sing. The sound was low and melancholic. Trips to the outside loo were terrifying, the ghost of a moon on the water broken by the current running to the bathing steps, or the wind whining like a kennelled dog under the bridge. Dord would stand by the balustrade keeping guard. She carried a pocket torch that she ran over the rocks, the faint beam no match for the dark. A more powerful flashlight had once been dropped by a sister into the thick seaweed beneath the loo. It settled deep underwater and remained shining gloomily there for a whole week while the battery ran low. The sea was deep and hungry and we had a pact that entitled us to wake the other under any circumstances.

Mor-mor's room – then our parents' – was directly below the dorm. Mamma was always the last one awake, to check that the valves of the gas cooker were switched off, sneaking from her bedroom with a candle when she heard the final slamming of a door signalling all had retired for the night. And she was first to rise, woken by the low chattering of the gulls, when the flushed light of early dawn filtered through Mor-mor's curtains tinting the wood interior with rose. Gazing at the islands of the Pacific Ocean that were printed on the burnt sienna curtain-fabric soothed Mamma after her short night. She liked this peaceful time, when Pappa might go deep-sea fishing for mackerel and she had her own thoughts before getting breakfast ready. She made preparations for a Mor-mor-style *dyne* morning, spreading herself out by the sauna as the sun crept up the left arm of the rocks and over Seagull Island.

A *dyne* morning was one of the defining episodes in the Småhølmene day, connected with all that could provide comfort in this world. Mamma breakfasted off what she called 'mother's mess', an ultimate muesli mix. It was really a bowl of pure creaminess, made somewhat less guilt-inducing with the healthy additions of oats, nuts, dried fruit, honey and a few precious island raspberries. She was a great espouser of the health-giving properties contained in certain dairy products. In London, she made yoghurt from a starter called Boris, given to her by a dog-walking friend who came from St Petersburg. Mixed with boiled milk, then left in the airing cupboard overnight, the indomitable culture produced pots of rather sour, viscous live stuff that still makes my sister Sasha shudder thinking of it. Mamma could take spoons of mother's mess from a large teacup, feeling confident that it was doing her good, while attending to all of us. Lying on our stomachs peering into the underwater kingdom of the lagoon, with boards of bread and chocolate that counted as a good start because it was the holiday, we were perfectly content.

During this period of felicity our way of talking about the island was almost courtly: respectful, reverent and high-blown. In our vocabulary 'a Småhølmene day' meant a sunny-windy day – the perfect island day – and when we talked of 'Norway' we meant only our fraction of it. An island summer: it set us apart from our peers, shoring up the family bond.

❉

By the mid 1980s, the circle of Mamma's island acquaintance had contracted. Many of the characters of former
decades had been friends and contemporaries of
Mor-mor's, and their deaths either predated hers, or they
did not long outlive her. They had enriched life at
Småhølmene, both as visitors and talking points over the
supper table. Mamma spoke fondly of bygone afternoons
eating cherry and fruit cake with 'Commander' Antonson,
the whale-catcher, relating his wartime feats, and in-depth
discussions of eiderdown covers with Antonson's wife,
Inge. Mr and Mrs A. had kept the keys to Småhølmene and
were thanked for their trouble with jam and Scotch, to
both of which they were extremely partial. The closing of
dour Thorsen's provision bunkhouse in Høvåg had been
the cause of other forms of disappointment and regret, for
with that event came the loss of much to complain of, or to
laugh over. Gone was the freezer compartment filled with
ice cream that could tempt a whining child to walk; gone,
the shelves for Mamma to exclaim at for their dustiness,
and the pallor of Mrs Thorsen which seemed part and
parcel of the overall impression that the place needed a
good airing.

In their stead came a smaller, replacement troupe with
whom Mamma built strong friendships despite the long
periods we were away. Mostly they had children who were
the same age as Dordie and me for us to play with, enduring
long, hot games over which very little was said and less
achieved, that were redeemed by the half-time feasts of dark

buttered bread, wildflower honey and rhubarb cordial carried to the thick yellow gorse above the house. From there, we carried on games of spy, catching strains of distant conversation from the grown-ups seated at the back. Among Mamma's friends were Roland, who was the caretaker of Småhølmene, and his wife, Marianne, who had dry skin like a hazelnut shell. The two smoked roll-up cigarettes, bottoms glued to the deck's hot paving stones. They had four flaxen children ranging in age from ten down, so granting freedom to my brother and sisters, unless inclined to lazily direct a game of kick-the-can. My mother's second cousin, Peter, was an engine brain without whom it was certain that none of our boats would function correctly. He serviced the outboards over the winter and they came back humming with good health and a smart reminder of the importance of mixing a percentage of oil into the gasoline for the two-stroke. His wife – feminine, blonde and neat – ran her kitchen like Peter ran his mechanical workshop in Lillesand: both had surfaces so clean, you could eat off them.

If we had a distinguishing feature, it was our primitivism. That the Småhølmene set were far behind others in orderliness was tolerated and laughed about, and yet the hospitality exchange could be very humbling. Mor-mor's high standards of entertainment were a thing of the past. It became particularly apparent at table, where nothing ever went together. Our pantry was full of odd china, and producing a pair of matching candlesticks was quite beyond our capabilities.

At the homes of our friends, waffle stacks seemed to stand to attention and bowls of wild blueberries to glitter like tiny sapphires. Olga would have noted how everything had its right spoon, or correct serving vessel. She would have appreciated the ceremony, that nothing was chipped to lower proceedings, that there were lace tablecloths and napkins.

Indoors eating had none of the hazards or the attractions of eating under the open sky. We never knew how to say no to the outdoors. Whatever the weather, we braved it for our view over the Blindleia. Food got cold quickly so we sped through meals without a thought for table manners. There was real freedom in this but it was not civilised.

Norwegians live by the maxim there is no such thing as bad weather, only bad clothes. All around us, people – islanders like ourselves – seemed to manage better, whatever the weather, still to keep up appearances. At Småhølmene, we only had fair-weather wear and so were underprepared for everything else. And because we were socialising less, we really let ourselves go.

A decade before my own island summers were to commence, when summer socialising was at its zenith, Mamma proudly recorded in her diary what she and her children had worn to celebrations at Akerøya in honour of Great Uncle Alfred's birthday. Everyone was kitted out in best bib and tucker. Mamma was clad in a silk shirt, waistcoat and jeans. Thomas found an outing for the Fred Olsen tie his grandmother had given him, paired with a white training-suit jacket. Sasha had worn bermudas and Emmie a red velvet short-suit. Of course Mor-mor had always been *kuste*, immaculately turned out. Even her casual had style. But gone were the days.

A Norwegian phrase, *slaskete klær*, meaning slovenly or unkempt, was now the holiday keynote. We lived in swimming costumes and shorts, with *lusekofte* for insulation. We gave suitcase space to useful things, *dyne* covers and towels, and in such number that we could just about get away with not having a laundry machine for the whole summer, hand-washing smaller items and pegging them out to dry in the wind. Such an airing infused clothes with a sweet, elusive island smell that married all the wild plants with sea spray and wood.

❋

Claiming ownership of the island felt almost absurd, like saying that all the wind, or earth, or water of the world was ours. So much of its surface tended towards the untamed and the wilderness-like that it could seem a place unfit for human interference or possession. Mor-mor, for all that she was a stickler for the finer things in life, valued this tension highly.

It would of course have been quite possible before 1985, when she died, to have modernised with the times. It was Mamma's private collusion in Mor-mor's vision of the island as somewhere without pretensions to anything smart or worldly that prevented her from making core changes. Mamma had taken on the running of the place single-handedly. Her siblings, though fond, could see its drawbacks and relinquished their share. With tributary lightness of touch, Mamma left everything just as it was. Practical improvements would have relieved her of some worry and made life in many respects much easier; for our pragmatic Norwegian friends, hard-wired to confront nature rather than simply submit to it, it was incomprehensible why we did not make them. There was a degree of wilful ignorance in failing to equip ourselves properly for the fact that nature could at times be hostile when thus exposed. It meant we often needed rescuing. Yet Mor-mor and Mamma were reverential about nature and Småhølmene represented its essence, in unfettered glory. Mor-mor designed island living on foundations that were romantic, and it was to continue so through Mamma.

We were haunted by Mor-mor's anti-engine and anti-gas feelings. Wood-burning was considered both extravagant and rather daring, meaning the house was almost never heated. Terrified that it might burn down, we would rather have endured a rainy night without a fire. A Jotul stove was bought, and installed, like a little footstool, before the open hearth. When the stove was lit, we imagined seeing tiny wispy emissions escaping from brickwork, or sneezed with the dust because the flue was so seldom used. Another of Mamma's diary entries, also from the 1970s, reads: 'Out of nearly all provisions. Akerøya crowd appeared, obviously annoyed and shocked by our Spartan life and only too pleased to hurtle back to deep freeze, electricity and Brekkestø's supermarket!' Though such a contrast could shame, it could never spur the installation of electricity, or flush loos, with us.

A Laboratory of Vikings and Sisters

Småhølmene drew us together where home concerns pulled us apart, and provided an opportunity for me, the youngest, to study the characters of my intriguing older brother and sisters. The isolation provided laboratory conditions to undertake my research. It accentuated what was fine in our natures, as well as shedding light on what was doubting, irresolute or nervous. Differences as well as similarities were discovered through being there. And though I saw all the older girls in the heroic mould, unstoppably great and good, it was evident that, while they might speak as one, there were areas that made them quite unalike.

Mamma's eldest daughter, Sasha, could give Latin names to all the plants of Småhølmene, knew the properties of island seaweeds and all the species of lichens covering the rocks. She was a botanical whizz, reading countless books on the subject and making pretty watercolours of sea thrift and campion. (She would go on to work at Kew Gardens, specialising in Phoenix palms.) She loved to

112

drink coffee, so that Pappa, who sympathised with and shared in her caffeine addiction, took to clambering carefully, cup in hand, to find Sasha sketching on a secluded boulder with pencils and a knife for a sharpener lying beside her on the rocks. Her drawings had such fine precision that I wanted my own to be just like them, accompanying her on some of these long outings, rubbing out as busily as I put anything down. She was a dab hand at *kaste sluken*, Mor-mor's special Småhølmene method of fishing, standing quietly on the far rock, enjoying the view. She was so well practised a thrower she scarcely needed to take her eyes off the horizon, where the outer skerries met under the sky. She said it was her favourite place on the island, arriving there by a daring route that took her as close to the water as the island geography permitted, never allowing herself a backwards step and going as fast as she possibly could. She almost always came back with cod, which shows how very patient she was: none of the rest of us could stand still long enough to catch a fish that way. Where we splashed noisily into the water, Sasha edged in with scarcely a gasp, as if it would betray the lagoon to make a sound.

Next came Emmeline (also called Emmie, or Em), who was physically very like Mamma to look at, so that, in the uncertain shifts of my early island memories, sometimes it is she who sits in the Hardanger and rows me around the island. She had strong arms suggestive of a mighty tennis forehand and was constitutionally robust, with a strong stomach, again like Mamma, who frequently volunteered to eat the first mussel of the season in the knowledge she would be able to soldier on even if it were poisonous.

Emmie understood the importance of providing entertainment to pass the hours and hours we had to fill on the island, thinking up diversions for Dord and me such as towing us behind *Little Thomas* on inflatable mats, every tug of the oars bringing a fresh cold sweep of seawater over our bellies, making us shudder with glee; or, when our hair was long enough, combing out all the tangles left by the sea-salt residue to braid in neat French plaits. I valued all intimations of equality and earnestly believed I was transcending the years of separation when she showed an interest. Emmie was the tour de force behind our special, exotic menagerie of parent-sisters. She could be a stern disciplinarian, something I remember in storyboard as being chased, pinned down and mercilessly tickled under the auspices of her checking whether I had cleaned my teeth or not. She saw the world in black and white, while the rest of us saw mainly greys. In this she was more like Mor-mor. Em inherited from her a great instinct for design, and spent one winter embroidering a cushion cover of a red lobster for the sitting-room using a pattern she found in Liberty's haberdashery department.

Rebecca Maria, girl number three, was named after the wild wind, *Maria*. And like the wind, you wanted her behind, not against, a point you were arguing. She was passionate, fighting for what she believed was right, fighting eventually and with untold force for us to keep the island. The Olsen gene has always been strong in her. As youngest of the first brood, Becky was close enough in age to Dord and me to feel some empathy for our wants. She made us indulgent chocolate biscuit cakes, using dried fruit and nuts from the hanging baskets in the kitchen, which she was tall enough to reach. She instructed us in backgammon and hearts. She was the spitting image of her grandmother, with a strong round face and freckles on her nose. Her hair and eyes were a lovely dark brown and her figure seemed cast almost exactly in the Mor-mor mould.

Even to a casual observer it would have been unmistakable that the three were sisters. Dordie and I, however, were more of a challenge. Peering into the looking-glass, I concluded that I was dismally foreign. My hair was much lighter. My eyes were the same washed-out green as the old glass jar of cardamom pods for stewing apricots. I was not beautiful like Dordie, with her distinguished Roman nose, and beauty spots on her cheek in the exact same pattern as the Big Dipper, part of the constellation of Ursa Major. But we two were more alike, cementing the sisterly bond between us.

I took heart at the thought of kinship with my half-brother, Thomas, for, like him, I was tall and metabolised food quickly. He was very slim, though with the sturdy Bennett bottom trunk. Each morning he made a dash for the *brygge*, dived and swam several times across the lagoon and back before devouring a colossal breakfast of muesli and buttered bread. He had Beste Pappa's integrity and work ethic – that was plain enough. He was responsible and good-hearted, as were his friends. I loved their visits to the island, the merry way they had of singing songs as they charged over the rocks on a mink ambush, or picking up rubbish that had washed ashore during a storm, all under Thomas's direction. On gramophone evenings, they danced with me standing on their feet, swirling me around so dizzily to a crackly 'Buttons and Bows' or 'Mac the Knife' that the sun and the ox-blood-red hut became a blur. Following the laws of primogeniture, Thomas seemed, being the eldest as well as the only boy, the natural inheritor of the island; he was always active in its preservation and did much towards its upkeep.

But we were all active preservers. From this came our family unity. Every interest and hobby in Norway seemed both to instruct, and to delight. Educated in setting proper value on what we found around us, we never missed what the island did not have, from sulky teens down to island ingénues, Dordie and me.

On sunny days, Mamma encouraged what she called 'exploring' in lieu of natural history. Sasha would school us in the names and properties of island flowers, which we brought back to the house for her inspection and then pressed between heavy books. That was botany. For astronomy we learnt to stargaze with Pappa pointing out the constellations of the northern hemisphere. I looked out

keenly for the Seven Sisters, redolent of our own domi-
nantly female family structure, with each individual star
shining modestly, yet together burning as powerfully as a
meteor. There was the constellation of Leo, my sun sign, so
worth spotting too. I begged to be furnished with pocket
books to identify sea plants, fishes and shoreline birds.
To name a thing is a sure path to feeling attached. I soon
became deeply so to the creatures of Småhølmene, even
the mink, in which I took a half-fearful, half-worshipful
interest which I thought zoological.

On the wild distant rocks we discovered mink droppings, egg-shells stolen from the seagulls' nests, and
feathers and bones from an older bird-kill. A sighting
across the lagoon could unsettle an entire afternoon. The
old binoculars were fetched from the sitting-room caddy
to scan over rocky boulders and the sea, for the mink was
amphibious, projecting the field still wider. A large stone
menhir that made the entranceway to the left arm of the
island had gained a reputation among the family as mink
territory. To traverse it was to confront the terrifying
possibility that an animal might have burrowed into the
ledge where one slid one's feet. Mink are aggressively
territorial. The thought alone could make us lose our
balance, for it was a complicated system requiring
leaning against the rock and shuffling along to safety on
the other side.

If island life taught one thing it was that man and beast
must live together in harmony. Only once was Pappa

forced to administer the death blow to a mink when it audaciously ventured into the house. Otherwise there was a strong feeling among us that the creatures of Småhølmene earned their right to live there unharmed. It was a hard life for them. Some perfectly innocent creatures lost their battle with life for no reason, like the fledgling gull, Baby Jesus, which Mamma eventually disposed of at the tip on the mainland, rowing with funereal solemnity to Bliksund and back again. After I had trailed about with the carcass under one arm for days I suspect she hoped that I would come to my own conclusions about death. But my understanding on the subject remained underdeveloped, for Småhølmene suggested itself as a land of miraculous renewal, or rebirth.

The smooth great black-backed gulls, for instance, which overwintered at Bitte Småhølmene, seemed to manifest continuities that defied death, the laws of age and inheritance. Precisely when the small island kingdom was nested on by a new generation, it was impossible to say. One summer's adolescent gull, a most unpromisingly fluffy custodian, had at some unfixed time to take over the kingdom as birthright. The natural patterns and cycles of the island, even from very early on, could give the uncanny feeling that time had somehow failed to pass.

As if in collusion, not a clock was found working at Småhølmene. If we wore a watch, we dived into the sea and forgot that it was not waterproof. When we emerged, we found the glass frosted over so that we could no longer tell whether the hands were moving or had stopped. In the sitting-room, a beautiful painted-glass wall clock served a purely ornamental function. Pendulum and cogs gleamed through the coloured pane as though at any minute they might whirr into action. The clock hands rested at midday, or midnight. A sister playing a trick on Dord and me, who could both be very gullible, would move the hands overnight and say Mor-mor's ghost had made the time change. Our gullibility extended to believing promises that we would or could be timed accurately fetching a forgotten book at the Velvet Steps, or retrieving sun block from upstairs for a tanning sister. The minutes and hours trickled into long summer weeks. After a while we found ourselves unable to recall what day it was, with no daily newspaper or radio to nudge us. This had the effect of making my early summers at Småhølmene seem one long history, without intermission, or chapter break.

What did stand out on the island was any unusual display of weather. Predating my time there were three memorable weeks of rampaging westerly wind, when the family had stayed in the house, dirty and constricted, desperate to be outside, but thwarted at every attempt. The wind had pushed against the stable-doors discouragingly and the windowpanes rattled in the frames. As well as a frequently despairing commentary – 'Wind getting us down with its never-ceasing whoosh!' – Mamma made an almanac of the wind force for every day of the holiday. How she measured this I have no idea. The pressure needle on the barometer switched inadequately and often seemingly arbitrarily between *Pent* (fair), *Utrygt* (unsettled) and *Regn* (rain). With its nautical air, the barometer, like the stopped clock, made fine decoration. Both were dictionary objects of Småhølmene, part of our island lexicon.

❈

My generous memory grants to each early summer endless sunshine. In truth, there were the mongrel days, when the weather could shift from morning to afternoon, so that a bright beginning would end up cloudy, or even with a terrific electric storm. There was so much sky to witness the changes. Mor-mor said that Småhølmene had a microclimate. Insofar as we were never quite aligned with what a place so very near as Høvåg was doing weather-wise, she appeared to be quite right. When it was raining over the mainland, the outer islands were basking like reptiles in sunshine. Adaptability was the key.

The shifting skies determined our occupations so that what had been a morning of indoor pursuits became an afternoon of almost frenzied outside activity. When it had rained hard, Dordie and I, in oilskin jackets, shorts and gumboots, with chocolate in our pockets, might bail out the boats simply for the fun of boarding each like a pirate, climbing from one to the next without setting foot on the *brygge* between, or practising the knot called the two half-hitches. And after the rain it was always a good time to fish. We might set off in *Little Thomas*, just us two, watching the light change on the water as we dangled our lines up and down. For children, the pleasures that the island afforded came with no tax added, and time there was on our side.

The Upstairs Double

The first sign that summers might not always be the same, with the full family retinue in tow, came quite early on, as my brother and sisters began to distribute the weeks of the holiday between the island and visits to friends with houses in the sun, or travelling off their own bat to faraway lands. By the second half of the 1980s, when the little town of Lillesand received the official stamp of a coat-of-arms depicting three anchors, symbolising its maritime and naval interests, they had reached, or were approaching, their twenties, and the call of India and the Himalayas, unimaginably foreign, sometimes took them away for complete island seasons so that Dordie and I could not even look forward to a late arrival. I for one was confounded by the idea that anything could beat a Småhølmene summer, though it was perfectly natural that the guests who came to our shores might expect a return visit paid them. I blamed these tempters wholeheartedly, serpents in the garden, unwilling to entertain the thought that my siblings might themselves wish to holiday elsewhere.

The staggering of their visits was not without its compensations. Dordie and I packed up the pokey dorm, emerging, like moles from a dark tunnel, with bundles of clothes and bedding to move across the landing into the upstairs double. Here was a change. The room was light and airy, with windows east over the lagoon, and west over the Blindleia. It was almost as good as being outside, since we were roused by the crying of the seagulls and the pelt of the wind. In the midnight hours, I tore through the collection of children's adventure stories left at Småhølmene: W. E. Johns's *Biggles* series with dashing pictures of the airman on the jackets, and *ex libris* stamps inside bearing Thomas's name; plus of course endless Enid Blytons, both the *Malory Towers* books and *The Famous Five*. Such reading led me to embellish aspects of island life: soaring seaplanes, late-night signals flashing from a boat, instances of childhood bravery. It lit my imagination and conditioned the games Dord and I would play the next day, games of smugglers, island rescue – and boarding school.

There were seldom any new additions to the island library. The ancient sawhorse in the *Kongeveien* loo, which took the overflow from bedroom shelves, was crowded with books and magazines. There were Mor-mor's murder mysteries and a collection of old *National Geographic*'s saved by Mamma. She was a keen amateur geologist and had gained membership of the exclusive Royal Geographical Society in London by declaring herself to be an expert on Scandinavian rock formation. Really there was far too much of the romantic in her to countenance scientific accuracy.

Mamma preached the old mythologies of Høvåg and the southlands. The local area wove fact and fiction into history and myth, some merely from the war years, others as deep and old as the forests. When the mainland was denominated an Area of Outstanding Natural Beauty, Mamma continued to call the swathe of tree-thick hills 'the head and beard of the troll'. Deprived the ring of official-dom, magic settled again over the scene. She told us of the *smånisse*, a mischievous little elf with a taste for porridge, and the story of the *Troll Grytte* – the Troll's Saucepan – a deep natural well in the rock on the way to the boathouse at Småhølmene. As a child, she had loved playing there, watching the birds settle around her, or spying out the goings-on at the house. Then one day it filled with rain-water that never evaporated. Dordie and I skirted it widely on our way to see if jellyfish had run aground on the slipway from the boathouse into the lagoon in low water.

Building up a transportable sense of Norway became of consuming importance for me, a sort of compulsive game to try to remember the essences of Småhølmene when I was away over the winter. The tastes and smells had to be imagined, because nothing was the same anywhere else. The musty fragrance of the untreated wood rooms, like the pages of an antiquarian book; the silken tug of the seaweed coming into Little Bay after swimming the lagoon, and the feel of the smooth hot rocks against bare skin; close-ups of sea thrift and island raspberries, so small they dissolved on the tongue; and the long views out to the horizon with the grey-and-black watchtower for ships to navigate by: the higher the definition of the picture in my mind's eye, the more the island seemed like a precious touchstone I must carry with me to test out friends. Until they had come themselves they might only estimate, and never fully grasp, its value – but by showing themselves appreciative of the idea they would be raised in my estimation, and I in theirs. All who were to love and understand us must see the appeal.

Nevertheless it could sometimes be hard to convey to the uninitiated the fully glory of the place – what made Mor-mor say 'bliss' every time she edged into freezing water, what made us venture north in summertime. If my picture of Småholmene was projected to the wrong sort of audience, it could then face a counter-claim that it was attached to a land that was cold and dark and even inhospitable. I simply didn't have the facts to argue. We seldom left the island and saw little else of the country. How far the real north was removed from our island idyll I could only guess. I was thus susceptible to any attack, whether local or generalised. The Norwegian landscape, our part of it, was rugged, that was true. Looked at in a certain mood, both the towering rocks and long sea views had a rather melancholic character. They were not sights to uplift in dejection. The light could be preternaturally strange. I grew afraid of the candles adrift on the windowpanes at night and believed a classmate who told me Norway was a land full of witches.

Did this affect my appetite for the place? Not really. We wore our heritage proudly and never more so than when we were in England, where my family seized every opportunity to show off its Nordic roots. I wore a dirndl for the school photograph and sang 'Santa Lucia' at the Christmas assembly. An enlarged photograph showing a bird's-eye view of Småhølmene, looking more than ever like a horseshoe, hung in the blue bathroom at home. We dared the disapproval of the masses by being as Norwegian as we could and liking it.

From a family with a history in language campaigning, it was a strange oversight that Mamma had not taught any of her children to speak Norwegian. Often she conducted telephone conversations to her own siblings in Bokmål to stop herself getting rusty, or because she wanted to have a secret communication. My brother and sisters and I littered our talk with pidgin Norwegian, island words secreted over the long summer. It flowed between us like nonsense verse. The accent was not difficult to mimic, with its grand rolling 'r's and diving syllables – we almost sounded plausible. And while we played such games, Mamma frequently gave English words a foreign intonation, or identified supermarket items by their wrong names, calling wraps *'potetmel pannekaker'*, or for scones, *'bøller'*. We were very confused. The island was run colonial fashion, with anglicised tastes and habits informing everything from the music we listened to and the books we read, to the times we ate at. We shunned the local habit of taking the main meal of the day in the late afternoon – *middag*, often the only hot meal, with *aftens*, a light snack before bed – so that any invitation given or received posed threat of a social faux pas.

❋

Mamma's wider vision of the island had always encompassed Akerøya as an extension of her closest family circle. It was the place where she sank most comfortably back into a complete Norwegian self. There she guarded that most priceless treasure: a position and function independent of her children. In the early years of her child-rearing, exchange programmes ferrying cousins back and forth between houses for spaghetti suppers and, at Småhølmene, camp sleeping quarters, had allowed some escape from parenting duties. Now, with a relaxed sense of obligation, she really let herself go, gossiping to her great ally and supporter Great Aunt Helle, joking with Great Uncle Alfred, paying Pappa very little attention and totally ignoring Dord and me.

Our favourite haunt was the observatory on the island tor, the very same where Mor-mor had once debated whether to purchase Småhølmene. Here we could play with little chance of being missed before the time of departure. On the sea approach, its windows caught the sun and gleamed brightly. It had a green domed roof and white panelled sides. Inside, there were stars painted on the ceiling with a midnight-blue background. The air was stuffy with old cigar smoke and the faint reek of brandy. In the evening, it was used as a *fumoir*, with the family climbing the hill after supper to sit in comfort and watch the moon rise over the water.

By daylight, an aerodrome of wasps created a buzzing sound that was soporific and Dordie and I lay watching them, blinking against the brightness of the sky. Giant ants marched over our fingers in single file, and flies landed on our legs, which we were too lazy to swat.

Then we crossed the bay, half walking, half skipping to the fisherman's cottage. It was another sort of pleasure we sought there. Marit, the fisherman's wife, approached the subject of afternoon tea with great seriousness. She honoured our visit with a buckling table. There were cream buns, waffle stacks and iced cakes. The array set forth brought on the full unleashing of our greed and we began an unspoken competition as to who could eat most. Småhølmene was governed by a spirit of restraint and to ignore it was slightly to disgrace oneself. Profligacy there lay in a lazy pour of milk to drown a bowl of porridge, or the thick lick of butter on a slice of bread. The labour even of buying necessary provisions took a whole morning, never mind wanton little luxuries such as our appetites craved. So we really went for it, delighting our hostess with our good appetites.

Marit had marmalade-ginger hair and she was a great talker. Having married with a mainlander's suspicion that island life might not afford much in the way of entertainment, she had looked forward to the arrival of her first child to provide her with valuable occupation. As it turned out, over the winter of 1979, when she nursed a new daughter, there was a deep sea freeze. She bore witness to winter's cadaverousness. The Antarctic explorer Ernest Shackleton, surveying the wreckage of the ship *Endurance*, which had run aground in pack ice short of Elephant Island on the Imperial Trans-Antarctic Expedition, 1914–17, once said: 'What the ice takes, the ice keeps.' Dredgers were stuck, frozen on a polar horizon, and the strange flat shapes of the outer islands looked like seal pups stomaching along the ice. The Brekkestø shop ran out of all supplies and she and Kay had to skate to the mainland to collect provisions from Marit's parents, with their baby wrapped tightly in the folds of a sling. She could not have asked for a more thorough-going initiation into the hardships of island living.

I begged to be told this story again and again, since the Norwegian winter was a blind spot in our Småhølmene repertoire. A sea freeze became the stuff of fantasy, a Narnia under the spell of the White Witch. Marit herself had a way of seeming excited by the chat, talking fast, rarely coming up for air, and making wilder and wilder gestures. Kay meanwhile was very peaceable and smiling. Though he spoke almost no English – this made him all the more Mamma's property – I found myself often staring at him, for he had a kind, encouraging face. He had apple-rosy cheeks and the crown of his head was smooth and shining as an apple that has been rubbed on a trouser pocket.

Dordie and I were allowed to explore his boathouse after tea. The place was musty-smelling, like sweet sherry mixed with blood. This, I felt, was a proper working boathouse smell. There was always a lot to look at: huge hooks hanging from nails in the walls, fishing nets draped over the rafters, and the hooped skirt of an eel trap. At one of Great Uncle Alfred's birthday parties, I had listened to Kay and his fishermen friends sing sea shanties there late into the night, perched on a stack of crab pots. I didn't want to move for fear they would ask me to sing. I was not to get off so easily. I was heckled until I delivered a few verses of 'My Bonny Lies over the Ocean' to rapturous applause.

After the party was over, we had congregated on the *brygge* to be driven back to the island along a moonlit Blindleia. Night-time voyages were very special. We always travelled to Akerøya in *Nico*, a beautiful wooden boat, varnished mahogany with a sky-blue tarpaulin rain cover, which folded back like an open car so that we could lie back and look at the stars. She had an imperious horn-blast that Dordie and I took delight in sounding when Pappa held up departure with forgotten goodbyes. Any older sisters who were with us assembled on the boat's snubbed prow. I envied them, though not as much as I might have, since below there was a latched compartment properly meant for buoys and anchors and spare engine parts, but which was always left empty so that a couple of stowaways could squeeze inside. Dord and I, when our eyes were tired with stargazing, preferred to travel stowaway class to any other, with the doors shut behind us and the engine rumbling.

Once we had even slept overnight in *Nico*, moored at Småhølmene on a starlit August evening. It was like camping in the garden, close enough for rescue not to be terrifying, but an adventure nonetheless. We read books by torchlight and listened to the lapping of the water as it ran gently against the boards, until we were rocked to sleep by the motion it created. In the morning, we had fiddled with the engine dials and let out the inevitable horn-cry to rouse the troops from sleep.

Sakte Fart!

From Småhølmene, the sea route to Kristiansand is about eleven miles, taking just over two-and-a-half hours one way without breaking the speed limit. (We were not above being amused by the signs on the waterway that read *Sakte Fart!* – Slow Speed! – but were far too law-abiding to go against regulations.) I remember our voyaging there only once and it was a real event. We piled into *Nico* wearing swimming costumes, shorts and dock-side shoes. Mamma sat at the helm on the red leather pilot seat, a hand resting on the tiller, nodding hello at passing boats. Trips along the Blindleia had an air of sociability to them. It was like going for a walk in the country, providing an excuse for the convivial scrutiny of others. Little gulps of seawater spewed from the blowhole in the boat's flank, as though she was puffing with the effort of carrying us all. I pitied the owners of the uglier gin palaces and ubiquitous motorboats, feeling confident that no one could fail to admire a craft as charming as ours.

When we arrived in the Kristiansand peninsula we found space to dock and Mamma was off, rushing around the shops buying swimming towels and nightshirts, knitting patterns and skeins of wool. She always liked to have what she called 'a winter project', which she accomplished in England, with island thoughts. The patterns and wool would travel home with us to give occupation as the nights drew in. Christmas presents were stiff Norwegian jumpers or cardigans with bulging shoulders and tight wristbands; Mamma had even found a design for a woollen swimming costume, which she threatened to make for us one day.

She was a smart home economist, mainly because of her genuine liking for being physically busy. In the afternoon sun, she would put aside her summer reading and use the daylight to work by. She was lost, often for hours at a time, to the 1930s Singer treadle, the advent of which meant remembering spare cotton reels and bobbins and needles, besides needles for the gramophone, before leaving for the holiday. Mamma whirred out cushion covers to adorn the sitting-room window seat, cutting the fabric carefully with pinking shears and keeping any spare in her work basket. She hemmed curtains for the washroom and sewed colourful mismatching ribbons on to *dyne* covers to brighten up the dorm. It seemed there would never be projects enough. But somehow, Mamma always found things to do by inventing where opportunity fell short. And when there had been a fabric surplus, Dordie and I would find dresses lying on our beds that matched something upholstered, which we hoped beyond hope to be able to leave at the island when we returned to London at the end of the season.

I left Kristiansand proudly clutching a toy fjord pony with a bristly hog mane as a souvenir. This was a delicious novelty. In Lillesand, shopping trips were military exercises, every halt planned for and the most direct route mapped out between them, so there was no scope for buying inessentials. Mamma was always most impatient to be back at the island again, so she took some trouble to draw up a list before setting out, to keep things as quick and efficient as possible, counting leftover cartons of milk under her breath and lifting the hatch to the storage space below the cooker where we kept potatoes, carrots and onions, to check supplies. The thrill of going off-list in Kristiansand had held Dord and me in agonies of indecision before shelves of model trolls and elk-skin pencil cases.

We stopped for an ice cream before departure, and I was holding what remained of a strawberry cone with one hand and schooling Pony along *Nico*'s varnished mahogany sides with the other, when the toy slipped from my grasp and was swirled around in the wake as we joined the busy Blindleia. I cried out for Mamma to turn back, a complicated manoeuvre when there were boats on all sides. After a painstaking rescue mission, earning him the name Lifeguard, the toy was recovered, wrung out and put in the sauna to dry.

A Småhølmene sauna could smooth over many such hiccups, deflect attention from the untoward happening and might serve any number of practical uses as well. The washing-up was done with a pot of water warmed over the top stones, and the embers banished damp from clothes hung there overnight. Opening the door to the sauna the morning after was to meet a welcome burst of contained heat and, if the weather kept up wet, we might sit in there to clean our teeth. Knowing such small patterns of economy, the way to get things done by capitalising on an apparently isolated event in the day, was what distinguished us from guests. It was why it was difficult for guests to help: no one could imagine the lengths to which we went. Sasha put the kettle over the smallest ring on the hob so as not to waste gas and never put just one tray of potato gratin or whatever in the oven when she could cobble together and fit in two, making full use of the energy. Mamma spent an hour squinting at the pages of her novel before lighting any candles and barked at us if we left a door ajar when the fire was lit.

※

For two weeks over the summer of 1988, Isla and Clova Gladstone, friends from London day school, came to stay with Dordie and me at Småhølmene. They promised to be in every respect model guests. They holidayed usually on the wild, west coast of Scotland, so we hoped that they could not be disappointed by cold seas or fierce weather. We four girls took a bed each in the dorm, where we were woken one morning to the dull chime of raindrops on the roof tiles.

One of the effects of the rain is to make everything on the island look much darker: the rocks, which turn a sombre grey; the deeper, more sanguine red of the house; the sea, which almost blackens. The rooms are gloomy, all excepting the sitting-room, kept warm and light by a crackling fire in the Jotul. It is the one, the only place to sit in when it rains, and as the programme of available pursuits is gone through there is soon an inevitable conflict between sedate and noisy ones, the readers and the watercolourists pursing lips at the hustlers going hammer and tongs at a game of racing demon. It takes about two to three hours for true cabin fever to set in.

A cosy breakfast of chunky Norwegian bacon, cut from a slab, with eggs and bread fried in the pork fat, gave way quickly to a sense of oppression as too many people crowded into the sitting-room at once. Sasha had a friend staying too and she was looking out miserably at the rainy Blindleia. It was as good as a declaration of her need for entertainment, so Sasha was becoming increasingly desperate. Mamma suggested, as she always suggested when the presence of guests coincided with a need for activity, that we climb Videheia and have a sauna on return. This walk, up a steep incline near Brekkestø, was Mamma's trump card. We seldom ventured there, for it was a tricky clamber and required almost an hour's boat journey there and back again. It became a sort of Everest when we talked about it to the uninitiated, and thus could disappoint when they saw only blueberry forests and jutting rocks, which made the whole scramble rather hair-raising. But, grateful to be on the move, all left the sitting-room to fetch thick socks and jerseys, while Mamma wrapped sandwiches for the picnic at the summit that made the outing an occasion.

In the lower reaches of the forest, sunk back among trees, there lay an abandoned cottage, and Clova and I ran ahead of the walking party to inspect the cobwebbed windows and the paint peeling from the walls like strips of bark. The family all knew, and were inured to the fact, that somebody would be hiding behind the hut to give laggards a shock as they passed; but when Clova let out a stage howl as she appeared running from the thick undergrowth, her sister's shout of surprise echoed around the valley and was gratifyingly spine-tingling.

We stumbled our way towards the cap with the yellow-green stain of wet lichen on our hands from where we had pulled ourselves up a gully or stopped a fall. Bushes glistening with tiny blueberries quenched our thirst on the climb. And then it came, the view, spread out across water and rock: fir trees, log houses, flags and the wash of travelling boats. The air was clean, filling the lungs with a draught of piercing freshness. Seagulls hovered on the wind currents, very white against the grey cloud. We searched for the coordinate points to locate Småhølmene, but could see only the pea-green lighthouse beyond Akerøya, and the watch-tower out at sea.

❈

Back at the island, smoke was curling from the chimney of the sauna and the lagoon had flattened as the wind fell. It was really a luxury to be allowed to remain behind and Pappa had made the most of his peaceful, solitary time. The bad weather drove the large jellyfish in and they had collected around the *brygge*, where they spawned pale, voluminous clouds that split and gathered, leading to remarks about jelly-soup from Mamma as she docked the boat. We pulled off our wet things, changed into our bathing costumes and converged on the sauna.

It was usually Mamma who was the designator of what constituted the right sauna temperature, and the one who most loathed the wrong one; a sauna that was not hot enough, as she said, could have the opposite effect to the desired one of enhancing the mood, especially her own. With asbestos hands she piled the burner with extra logs as the flames licked out, and ladled water, scented with a few drops of pine, on the hot stones so that a hiss of aromatic steam came up, intensifying the heat. Standing back, she took a satisfied in-breath and shrugged the straps of her costume away from her shoulders. Round One went smoothly as the three guests, heeding warnings, successfully avoided being stung by king and queen jellies lurking beneath the bathing steps on the first swim. Back in the sauna, Isla and Clova retreated to the lower bench while Sasha and her friend, Dord and I packed in like sardines on the upper, dripping seawater on them through the slats. As we settled into Round Two, raindrops began to streak the porthole window. Disaster struck when, leaving for another dip, Isla took the *brygge* at a run, slipped, and fell headlong into a nursery of jellyfish babies. She braved the last round anyway, though her leg had been grazed in the fall.

A pot bubbled expectantly on top of the stove, and I urged on the moment when Mamma would lift it by the rim with a towel and carry it out to the *brygge*. There, it would be mixed with cold for a makeshift outdoor shower, and we took turns to pour jugs of the warm water over one another, looking out to Seagull Island. It was the crowning moment of any sauna, a moment that was almost euphoric as cascade after cascade drenched away goose-bumps and salt. The china wash-set that was reserved for the ritual – speckled duck-egg blue with bibulous purple bruises for grapes – had somehow remained in one piece through all its outings, though our fingers were always wrinkled like prunes from the sea when we handled it. Basin and ewer gave to proceedings a Victorian distinction. Even Sasha's doubting friend showed enthusiasm when, kneeling over the *brygge* with her hair full of suds, the first shock of warm water hit. Afterwards it was books, *dyner* and quiet time.

We were given ginger biscuits and mugs of hot cordial, for Mamma placed emphasis on the importance of rehydrating ourselves, and granted herself an hour or so of peace before the evening regained momentum.

Mackerel Skies

t some point, travel to the island began to take on a rather different slant. Perhaps Mamma had had enough of the arduous ferry crossings, or there was simply less stuff to take, with dwindling numbers of children. We flew out from Heathrow on Scandinavian Airlines, exploring the fascinating compartments of the meal-tray filled with salmon, Atlantic prawns and iceberg lettuce, and the baked bread rolls that filled the plane with the warm smell of yeast, and through which real butter melted in golden sundowns. A stopover in Oslo provided an opportunity for the first ice cream of the season. When Dord and I got bored of our puzzle books, Mamma handed us crisp kroner notes and gave instructions that we return in time to board the domestic shuttle service that would take us to Kristiansand, Kjevik. Soon we were wandering around the gates slurping *soft-is* and looking at the tanks of blue lobster by champagne and caviar bars, and at postcards of the land we were destined for, a place of wild cataracts, *fjell* and fjord.

Before take-off on the short flight to Kjevik, the SAS crew handed out to each child painted cardboard containers with animal crackers, jelly sweets and a small stuffed toy inside. I both longed for and dreaded the day I would outgrow this. Mamma sucked boiled sweets to stop her ears popping throughout the flight, her cheeks moving subtly as she leant her head back against the rest and shut her eyes. A nervous traveller, the turbulence over the Drangedal mountains made her pull her seatbelt tighter by a reflex. When we landed, Pappa lugged the bags off the carousel and we bundled into a taxi. The attractive coastal road gave a foretaste of the pleasures to come as we drove along rocky bays where brown families swam and sunbathed, through dappled woods verged by gleaming berry bushes and past the stone troll Kassen Tassen himself as we crossed the bridge to Bliksund, where the boat was moored.

Mamma was approaching fifty, so keeping fit and trim was top of the agenda. By folding everything else very neatly in her suitcase she found room for a few water aerobics floats – she took classes in London – as well as a skipping rope. Dord and I soon began an intensive regime of plain and cross-skipping on the Blindleia side, counting out a tally as we went for world records. This usually came to an end when I landed hard on a broken snail shell and had to leap into the lagoon, where the cooling salt water cleaned the cut.

In the sea, I beelined for Mamma, who was pedalling and punching the water, bits of aerobics gear floating around to be grabbed when needed. I dived and took hold of her legs, managing to keep up an assault of dummy shark attacks so that she eventually gave up and swam away towards the bathing steps. Like Mor-mor, Mamma found means to enhance her physical well-being through her love of nature, and her fondness for animals. In London, she walked in Kensington Gardens twice daily, long perambulations swinging her arms and breathing deeply with the dachshunds in tow. On favourite days, such as the London to Brighton car race, which had its beginnings in the park, she would vigorously push whichever of her offspring was still in a perambulator to watch the off. At Småhølmene, she missed this routine, but there were other forms of exercise, all demanding the sort of strength and vigour that toned out the body. Mamma prepared meals to combat the extra inches, cooking down whatever roots and greens she found in the store cupboard to make a sloppy and surprisingly delicious vegetable mess. After a number of weeks away, however, the fight for fitness-boosting told on her emotionally as well as physically. She could become what she called 'tissicky', unable to settle to anything, and depressed, a mood that lifted only following a good night's sleep.

❋

Childish moods, sunny and cloudy, and childish occupations, in only some of which I could persuade Dordie to take part, were still the essence of my Småhølmene summers. I would have it that she shared in them all, but she was embarking on the teenage years, with different feelings to my own. She had her ears pierced and wore little gold hoops in them like a pirate girl. I was a tomboy of the *Just William* school. William was my hero and role model. I took pride in my scuffed knees and wished for a band of outlaws with whom to share my adventures. I made catapults out of rowan twigs and pelted jellyfish with abandoned snail shells and pebbles from the Little Beach. Rock pools always fascinated with the starfishes and tiny crabs they housed, like mini aquariums. I scavenged pearly mussel shells from the rocks for Dordie to thread into a necklace, an occupation that took me past all sorts of exciting things on my way so that I came back with a rich collection of unusual bits of seaweed, or a broken bottle blown in from sea. Together we sometimes made rafts out of driftwood, all nails and uneven joinery, which we set afloat in the lagoon. Once the wood that we had collected dried, Dord and I began to saw, sand and hammer, invading Pappa's corner of the sail-loft to get the wherewithal.

For a man hard-wired for neatness and order, Pappa let the carpentry area become really dusty and messy. Where Mamma focused on domestic improvements, Pappa involved himself in heavy manual work, for instance building a large new table for suppers on the Blindleia side. It was weighty as a sacrificial stone and we dreaded the supports falling out, as they sometimes did over supper, when we hugged our knees up to our chests in terror.

On the lagoon-side wall of the sail-loft, a great assort-
ment of tools hung from rusty nails, while on the Blindleia
side there were shelves of varnish, outdoor paints and
brushes, and a sawhorse. Pre-war oilskins hung from the
rungs of a ladder in the beams, canary-yellow jackets,
waders and waterproof hats. Mor-mor's tartan-lined felt
fishing coat hung conspicuously among them, the colour of
dirty milk. It had peg buttons, like whale's teeth, and deep
pockets that I could store old shells in. It made me feel
invincible wearing it, though it hung off my small frame.
I was under my grandmother's protection, her apprentice
and inheritor.

When the rafts were seaworthy, Pappa was summoned
to the bathing steps for the maiden voyage. We watched as
they danced on the currents, and when a gust of wind
upturned one, dived into the water to set it back on course.
In this way we spent precious hours at the centre of Pappa's
interest and attention. To me, he fell into the category of
enigma. A competent and involved nanny, Veronica had
initially made both parents more like strangers, but
relations with Pappa, who was often away with work,
remained distant and insubstantial in the early years.
I granted him attributes of worldliness and life experience, so that I felt I could ask him anything – animal,
mineral or vegetable – and be certain of an answer. He
could tell me, for instance, that in the Wessex country,
where we sometimes spent the weekend, the upturned
stones where fields had been left fallow over the winter

were called 'forest marble', for they contained Jurassic-period fossils. I remember how he bent with real joy to look at the imprint of the pretty little seashells of unfathomable age. But there were emotional avenues with him you did not go down, unlike with Mamma, who had no gift for apportioning parts of herself but instead gave all.

Pappa and I shared some traits, mainly of appearance but also of character. I remained skinny and long-legged, requiring regular feeding, for I could become morose and silent when my blood sugar got low. Pappa also needed plenty of titbits to keep him going. Moderation lay in his foundations. He never ate or drank too much, but nor would he think of missing a meal. Bowls of bananas, cream and brown sugar, which Dordie wrinkled her nose at in disgust, were our regular, high-energy snack. We frequently breakfasted together in the Christmas and Easter holidays, when he fried eggs and bacon to give us a proper start for the day. Milk boiled for his coffee always stretched to a small cup of chocolate for me. It was when I felt most grown-up, the mornings Pappa and I would sit so quietly over our breakfast.

Pappa had been exploring in the boat when he discovered an ice-cream shop in Ulvøysund. On an especially nice afternoon we set out to try it, taking lines to fish with so as to make good use of the journey. Pappa knew instinctively the optimum speed for trawling from his motorboat, the *Lego Boat*. Unlike the rest of the island craft – the Hardanger, *Little Thomas* and *Nico* – it had a

Olga Olsen – 'Mor-mor' – in her early twenties, with dogs Ric and Ole in the Norwegian *fjell* (1930s). Always a great believer in enhancing physical well-being through outdoor exercise, she loved to walk and was an observant and ardent naturalist.

Charles Peto Bennett – Beste Pappa – takes the helm (1930s). Born to an English father and Norwegian mother, he and Mor-mor married in September 1935.

Despite all appearances, Mor-mor was a nervous sailor. She distrusted anything mechanical and when she was on her own preferred to row rather than use an engine.

Mor-mor and Great Aunt Helle catching the reflections of the sun on the water.

Beste Pappa and Sosse, Mor-mor's cousin and adoptive sister. The year
the photograph was taken, 1934, a large gang of friends were staying
at Great Aunt Helle's summer house on the island of Akerøya, in the
south of Norway. They liked to take Mor-mor's old, peacock-blue Decca
gramophone out with them on the rocks in the afternoons.

The Akerøya *paviljong*, or observatory, sits above the house on the island tor and boasts wonderful views. Here I imagine Mor-mor to have sat with Great Aunt Helle and Great Uncle Alfred after seeing Småhølmene – the Small Isles – for the first time, discussing the purchase.

Småhølmene under construction (1948–49). Though she hired an architect to draw up plans for the house, Mor-mor schemed out a large portion of it herself and oversaw some of the building. The cabin is timber-built with a low, curling tiled roof – the vernacular style of the area – and painted ox-blood red.

Mor-mor, contrapposto. She made a more formidable sight with the standard black poodle, Cheri, barking by her side.

Caroline Elizabeth Peto Bennett – Mamma – in oilskins with a tether
of rope (1950). The pre-war waterproofs ranged from canary yellow to
fireman's red, colour to be visible in the event of capsize. The originals
are still used by us today, the fabric being hard-wearing and durable.

Mor-mor coming to dock.

Mamma – here seven or eight years old – standing outside the cabin, proudly holding her catch aloft. Fishing was one of the essential skills she had to master as a young islander. *Torsk*, or north Atlantic cod, would always be prepared according to Norwegian custom: poached in salt water and served with boiled carrots and potatoes – with the addition of melted butter and a scattering of curly parsley to make it even more delicious.

Småhølmene's original buildings, cabin, sail-loft and *Kongeveien* (King's Road) bridge, with the addition of the Honeymoon room – behind the flagpole – which my father built as a surprise for my mother. The boathouse is on the far left.

Sasha and her friend in the upstairs double (1970s). This is the pre-scene to a '*dyne* morning', when we islanders congregate around the kitchen area with bedding and books. The first thought of the day, after listening for the sound of rain on the roof tiles, is whether it is actually sunny. Then decisions are taken as to whether a swimming costume, nightshirt or full oilskins are appropriate attire.

The only photograph of me with my grandmother (summer, 1984). My sister Georgina (Dordie) and I sit with Mor-mor on a typical *dyne* morning at Småhølmene.

Dordie, with seaweed, on Raspberry Island (summer, 1991). Rowing or swimming to Bringebærhølmen – Raspberry Island – is a favourite activity in good weather. The distance is negligible but the fun of marooning ourselves away from the central island never fails to inject new life into a party. It has sheltered nooks for picnics and inlets for swimming. There is also the appeal of being the first to spot the resident mink.

Me, in a fox-fur Russian hat in snowy Lillesand (2006). Spring had already begun to creep over England when my boyfriend Paddy and I left, heightening our sense of surprise to view the wintery landscape that greeted us.

Paddy taking me for a spin on the Blindleia (2006). We had no boat for the early part of our stay due to the thick ice which made transit impossible; with the thaw came greater freedom. We invented frequent excuses for an excursion, getting to know the surrounding islands with their foraging booty.

Enjoying tea on a sheepskin run in the afternoon, outside the Honeymoon room (2006). Despite being in a place outside of time, we were completely bound by ritual: breakfast, second breakfast (with coffee), lunch, afternoon tea, first drink, supper.

Småhølmene in late spring (2009), with juniper, lichen, rowan and mackerel flowers growing on the rocks.

Me on the top rock, wearing Mor-mor's jacket under
a mackerel sky (2009). From this vantage point there is a
wonderful panoramic view: Mamma's 'Head and Beard
of the Troll', the harbour master's house, the islands of
Trondarøya and Calvøya and the open sea.

Rowing on the lagoon. Since the winter stay, I have begun to crave the off-peak times most of all for my island visits, with the empty seas running into the horizon.

sleek modern finish, a powerful outboard motor and absolutely no character. Yet on stormy days when a Lillesand trip was necessary to replenish store-cupboard provisions, Pappa would take us in the *Lego Boat* on the outer sea route to the town at full throttle, and this journey always had us screaming with delight.

We rated speed more highly with every passing year, but trawling offered excitement of a different sort: suspense and the anticipation of the first bite. Pappa might appear relaxed and forgetful of our purpose, but he took care when steering that Dordie's and my reels should not cross over, looking over his shoulder to where they stretched out like washing-lines. He had reserves of patience that lasted right up until the moment a fish bit, when he would smack the engine into neutral, making us lurch forward, then grab the lucky reel and land the catch himself. Such was his haste he did not always bother to wind in properly, so the line had then to be untangled, which was fiddly and faintly nauseating work, tossed about on the waves.

If trawling is racing on the flat, then deep-sea fishing is like a steeplechase. Far out to sea, the rollers became like massive jumps, making my stomach disappear, and it was only by fixing my gaze intently on the rocks, and making shapes thereof, that I could keep from feeling sick. Any complaint and Pappa became silently irascible. Speed was of the essence when mackerel fishing: it was important to throw the line out again as quickly as possible to capitalise on being over a shoal. He taught us to interpret the oily, rainbow-coloured sheen on the water as a sign we were above one. 'Mackerel are the pigs of the sea,' he was fond of saying, with the satisfaction of an animal tracker who has found fresh droppings.

As we went in search of ice cream, a refreshing sea breeze blew away the cobwebs left over from a *dyne* morning at Småhølmene. I looked appreciatively around me at the villas and the neat wood huts, the boathouses and the deck bungalows with near-naked sun-worshippers draped on chairs outside, or somebody frozen at the end of a diving board, reluctant to leap. The scenes became a single thread, a story of the summer, and for once, I felt, we were all in unison, caught up in the indolence and activity of the season, no longer a family isolated; a family of solitary islanders, but part of a collective consciousness. Certainly it was plain from the queues of people lined up for ice cream that the whereabouts of the kiosk was common knowledge. This somehow encapsulated the August mood: everyone ate lots of ice cream in Norway. Soon I was licking the rivers of almond and vanilla running down the cone on to my fingers. Herring gulls hopped closer to where I sat, swinging my legs over the *brygge* – summertime was rich pickings for the birds.

On the return journey Dordie reeled in four mackerel on a single line, cleverly not telling Pappa until the moment they came up, silver gleams under the surface, so that she could do it all by herself. She became at that moment the heroine of the trip. Supper was fixed. As evening cast its spell over the island, she picked out her favourite record, Dinah Shore's 'Buttons and Bows'. The gramophone was becoming increasingly temperamental with age, so one of us had to be on hand to wind as the chorus began to fade. A jet of heat plumed into the still air as Pappa lifted the top off the barbecue to nestle salt-crust potatoes wrapped in foil among the charcoal. The window of the kitchen was pegged open and light was falling across it at a diagonal, so that the mackerel in dishes were formed of lapis lazuli and emerald.

Of fishy suppers Mamma held the greatest suspicion. A dextrous hand gutting cod and mackerel over the *brygge*, it was when they came, poached, fried or barbecued, to table that Mamma baulked. Haunted by memories of choking as a child, she had a pernickety deliberateness when removing bones, sticking out her tongue in concentration and peering closely at her helping. What she liked was crispy mackerel skin, boiled cod's cheeks and cod liver fried in butter, because all these were bone-free, and we transferred from our plates to hers those things which, to us, were a challenge, but to her were so delicious. She was also an enthusiastic taker of cod liver oil – a spoonful of which formed part of the 'Oslo breakfast' she remembers from girlhood, with a bowlful of full-cream Jersey milk, half an apple or a carrot, a wedge of mountain cheese and a slice of rye bread – attributing to that tonic her good skin, though not drinking or smoking must also have helped.

Pappa thus took charge of all fish cookery. He weighed as closely as the island measuring scales allowed how much salt was going into the pot for a proper saline water bath, or counted spoons of parsley for a reduced butter sauce. Culinary showmanship, outside the normal run of cooking, was where he shone. Mamma, on the other hand, used to feeding many mouths and in the early days being at the stove twice, if not three times, every school day, was a very efficient as well as a gifted home cook. And what she really excelled at was comfort food, making up for in taste what it lacked in presentation.

Mamma yielded to no one in her love of butter, eggs folded in creamed gold, sausages glistening with regular turning in the pan, waffles with pools melting in their grids so that the jam sat like islands surrounded by warm yellowy moats. Nothing was ever spiced, except for her one concession to cocktail hour: a tall glass of Clamato juice with dashes of Worcestershire Sauce and Tabasco. She usually hated any flavours that were briny or pickled, such as anchovies, olives and capers. Nursery suppers were her forte. As with all large families, at meals it was elbows out and feet in the trough. Plain Norwegian food suited Mamma's tastes. *Bøller, skolebrød* – literally school bread, an enriched dough bun with an injection of real vanilla custard, dusted with coconut icing – and the long strips of golden pastry containing soft raisins and cinnamon-spiced apple purée that oozed out with every bite: all these seemed designed for Mamma's special enjoyment. She sometimes gave way to temptation and polished off seconds of whatever happened to be left, turning her eyes to heaven and pleading for forgiveness and to be taught restraint.

Cholesterol and calories, neither of which I understood at all, were often talked of. Beste Pappa had suffered from high cholesterol and it seemed a matter that was genetic, rather than something for which cream could be held accountable. I did not want Mamma any other way than she was and bought her a birthday card with my own pocket money, which read: 'I wish I had been born before cholesterol was invented.' I found it inexplicable that she minded the soft angles that were exposed in the sauna, or while she was washing quietly on the bathing steps. Mamma was so naturally good-looking that I identified her unconsciously with some goddess: an Aphrodite married to a sun god. She was a prophet and sage too, interpreting the signs of the weather, understanding the small significances of a mackerel sky – the dapples, like a broken plane trail, meant unsettled weather to come – and what she called 'poodle clouds', converging in rosy banks over the lagoon-side view, reflecting the last rays of sun. These beauties were the final act to a storm. Days to come would be scalding, making the horseshoe-shaped island glow with fresh fire.

✸

The Raspberry Channel ran deep and blue until level with the house, where the bottom came up suddenly and the water turned a violent aquamarine before the weed, when it became silt green-brown. Over the warm days of summer, Dordie and I swam to and fro across the channel to Raspberry Island, carrying bits of picnic until a whole meal was assembled, to enjoy in solitude on the uninhabited land. Once we pulled ourselves up on the rocks we were soon dried off by the gentle gusts of the *solgangsvind*. This phenomenon occurred when the cool night air on the ocean met the heat of the morning, stirring a shimmering breeze that changed direction as though following the sun. The wind was briskest mid-afternoon when Bitte Småhølmene, the small islands on the Blindleia side of the house, seemed a fairytale kingdom protected by the waves. At dusk the wind stilled quite suddenly and the sea became a placid lake, full of mirrors. The water acted as an amplifier to the bird cries and shore sounds of wood being cut, or the bark of a dog.

The Honeymoon Room

I n the autumn of 1990, Dordie and I were sent to a
boarding school in the country to give Mamma time
off from being a mother and to concentrate on being a
wife. Locked in a closet world of make-believe and fantasy
games that drowned out all unwelcome sounds, Dordie
and I felt this only as a blow to life as we had known it, and
were not going to investigate it for the root cause: the
tremor in our parents' marriage that threatened some
dreadful eruption to come. There were wrenching adjust-
ments to make from an island summer to school life. The
claim that the first years' sleeping quarters, called Florence
Nightingale, were haunted seemed improbable, what with
all the starched white and hospital corners. I compared it to
our comfortably dusky and low-raftered, four-bedded
Norwegian dorm, which seemed the essence of what Enid
Blyton must have meant in her school stories – a place
made for midnight feasting, torches by the bedside to read
by and with a real lagoon to swim in on night-time adventures – then was constantly homesick. Dordie's patience

wore thin at nightly summons from the common room to comfort me after lights-out. I became a convincing skiver, though nobody was easier to convince than Mamma, for she would rather have had us both at home than not. Nor did Pappa put up any fuss when I returned in the car with them on Sunday nights to London, and thus missed a few more days of school.

Throughout that first term, Pappa was hatching a further plan to raft him and Mamma away from the big ship of the family, hoping by setting the relationship adrift to improve it. He was drawing up plans for an extension, a double bedroom and bathroom suite to adjoin the old house at Småhølmene. He often had a faraway look as he planned his surprise.

Island history was dead against it. Ever since Beste Pappa had felt his wife's pleasure in, and understanding of, Småhølmene, it had seemed a place set aside for female governance, and so to alter it in any way was a huge liberty. Certainly from Mor-mor's second marriage on, it had been a condition of occupancy that the island in no way belonged to partner or husband. She had been direct and combative in the assertion of her right to rule. With Mamma this happened obliquely – never by direct order, but in our mimicry of things she did, spoke or even felt about the island.

That Mamma knew Småhølmene best of all, that her identity and inheritance was bound up therein, influenced all of us. We peeled vegetables not in the kitchen, but over the *brygge*, shedding the curls of carrot or potato skin into the water, for that was Mamma's way. So too were the weeding parties at the Little Bay, to uproot the colonising Japanese knotweed, and toasting milk chocolate over a candle flame after supper to give it, if not a better, at least a more pronounced island taste. She could keep a single piece going until it was the thickness of a postage stamp, finally letting it dissolve on her tongue before starting another bit.

There was another reason for the planned development. Ever practical, Pappa had taken the cold hard fact of a need for more beds howsoever long my siblings and I were to summer on the island and discovered, quite characteristically, the only really viable solution. And, even for Dordie and me, at full-house the walls of the main building could seem paper-thin. Sounds carried, making every conversation that was not whispered a public statement. Our impractical thoughts on generating space had taken in Raspberry Island and Seagull Island, imagining the tiny little huts that could be built on them for still wilder living. Making the boathouse a sort of barn conversion also crossed our minds, while hoping never to fully banish the marine smells, or the sense of being afloat. Mor-mor's foundation structure and the eternal shapes of the islands forbade further imprint. All this simply meant Pappa had little difficulty in keeping his plan secret.

※

The approach of the winter holiday made the last weeks of term seem agonisingly slow and, when finally it came with its hurried collection of gym clothes and stuffing of trunks, our longing to be home had reached fever pitch. The house was decorated from the holly wreath on the front door and sprig of mistletoe hanging in the hall, to the rush-weave elves and pixies peering from the windows on to the one-way street. I loved the time of year and we went about all our usual traditions, walking past Harrods after dark to admire the Christmas window-displays and checking the Round Pond in Kensington Gardens with Mamma to see if it was covered in ice.

Then one day the parcel arrived containing little logs of dark chocolate-covered German marzipan in a celebration box, heralding in my mind the start of the joyous excesses. They came from a zealously remembering relation, and Mamma usually tore up the accompanying card guiltily, having forgotten to send one herself. The first chocolate always tasted the best, and we gazed on the trophy we held in our hands before thinking of putting it to our mouths. This was the real thing, marzipan containing 60 per cent nuts, and the rest sugar with just a little liquid – water, or brandy – to mix. The almond paste was sweet and crumbling, very slightly dry, and the chocolate so fine that it splintered like precious crystal with each bite.

There was always a big bowl full of nuts to shell on the kitchen table: tough-shelled Brazils, fiddly hazels, and walnuts like human brains. Best of all were almonds. When we cracked a shell containing two nuts, embracing so tightly they were shaped in beautiful symmetry, we gave one half to a sibling. Then we set a date on which we must remember to say, 'True Love,' and the first to say it would have luck and love for a whole year.

First thing on the twenty-fourth, Dordie and I stepped willingly into our childish Norwegian national costume, allowing Mamma to tie starched white aprons around our waists and pin brooches with tiny gold cymbals to the fronts of our dirndls. We had red Christmas ribbons in our hair, which she had cut in the usual square bob. We set off to Chelsea Square to be greeted by Great Aunt Helle wearing a dark turtleneck and gold chain and Great Uncle Alfred in velvet smoking jacket and Levantine slippers, both exuding antique powdered glamour. The drawing-room was oppressively hot, with a fire roaring in the grate, sending the Kerry blues and Yorkshire terriers into a decline around Alfred's feet. The parlour atmosphere was stifling to youngsters so eager to see the tree and open the presents. We slipped out and stole buttered bread and slivers of salmon from the sideboard in the dining-room where lunch would soon be served with aquavit, pinching bits of cucumber covered in sprinkles of dill with our fingers to go on top. We took this feast into the garden and ate it sitting against the trunk of a magnolia covered in snow. Dirndl material was very thick and we had finished long before the cold got into our legs.

Riȝcrem with an almond would come later on, when we congregated before the tree after a short rest. I liked the stodgy pudding much more than Dord, and so was always eager for that particular ceremony. But I had another reason to look forward to the ladling-out, hoping that I could somehow magic Emmie the lucky almond so that she would open the first present.

I took my first bowl of pudding with extra cream and cinnamon slowly, hoping I would not find the nut in my bowl. Mamma asked for a small spoon to make hers last longer. The smell of roasting goose and the twang of vinegar from spiced red cabbage wafted in, so that people began to declare they should never manage to do the Christmas meal justice as second helpings of rice were taken round. Then in what I interpreted as the divine fulfilment of my wish, Emmie let out an unsporting yell of glee as she spat the almond out on her spoon. I begged her to pick mine as the choice present and she sat by the tree prodding it for clues as to what was inside before she began tearing off the tissue wrapping.

Our small allowance of pocket money was hard to stretch to buy Christmas presents worthy of the sisters. Finally I had something to give that I felt sure Emmie would treasure. She had lost her favourite teddy bear, Arthur – named for his arthritic appearance – at a hotel in America, and I had found at an advent fair a similarly decrepit stuffed bear for a song. But, searching her face for signs of pleasure, I was shocked to see that she was crying. This was something I had not bargained for. I did not yet know tears could mean all sorts of things besides actual upset. Emmie was a sort of delightful wicked stepmother figure and it turned everything upside down to watch them roll down her cheek and to feel that I might unwittingly have been the cause.

Dord and I distributed presents while Mamma wrote a list of whom to thank. Emmie was smiling now with the success of the wind-vane in the shape of a whale that she had given Mamma, the colour of the sea on a stormy day. A gong was sounded, warning that the Christmas feast was moments away. Before the goose we ate *juletorsk*, Christmas cod, and because it was my first time tasting it I made a wish. I also took my first sip of juniper berry beer, called 'Christmas Champagne', passed to me like a libation by a sister.

❉

The spring and summer terms passed uneventfully. While my homesickness stabilised, my sibling regard was magnified by the long absences. I was cheered on by the thought of any approaching holiday, or half-holiday, because there was a chance they might be at home. Sometimes the elder girls picked Dordie and me up from school in second-hand cars, stalling as they inserted mix tapes, or filling us with sugar bought from petrol stations. 'Love you infinity,' coined by Em, with which we soon signed off all our school letters, encapsulated our feelings.

All were due to come to the island for at least a bit of the summer and I was exulting until I learnt that there would also be our cousins, Dinah and Saul. I felt mixed things about having to share my sisters, and Saul, who was more Dord's age than mine, was sure to claim her for the few short weeks when we were three years apart instead of two, after her but before my birthday. Dinah, another two-and-a-bit years older than Saul, nearly fourteen, was an unquantifiable threat, as I couldn't work out to whom she belonged; not to the older girls, who towered above, and certainly not to me, who shrank well below. As for Mamma, nervously preparing for all to run smoothly, more than ever impatient at the excessive number of bottles Pappa smuggled through customs for the celebration only he knew would be taking place, she was too preoccupied to notice, or for me to voice, my concerns. Aunt Magda was to come too, in part to shepherd her children, but also as a significant prop to the old-world Småhølmene. It was to be a return to the golden age.

The boathouse, because it hid what lay behind, acted as the curtain at the start of a theatrical performance. It seemed to sweep up, dramatically revealing the house, which puzzled, like a Rubik's cube, with strange new angles and confusing new shapes. Pappa had conducted us in from the Gull Channel, taking the lagoon turn wide and slow, so that it was moments before we realised anything was up.

Mamma's face changed from placid expectancy to confused shock, and then to a more pronounced look of surprise. Under her breath came an astonished 'Oy-oy-oy', a sound to which all the family resort in times of crisis.

Pappa, who had seen the finished building in May during a secret trip to the island, was the most collected.

He explained everything: that he had been the architect; that Peter Widmer had been a valued co-conspirator overseeing the demolition and early construction, and a necessary line of communication between Norway and England. The upside-down 'V' of the roof was set at a right angle to the old house. On both east and west pediment was a white-sash Diocletian window. Below, the ox-blood-red wood panels made the place look on the surface very like the original. But the doors – and there were two, one on the lagoon and the other on the Blindleia side – were not Småhølmene stable-doors, which could be swung open in halves depending on how friendly one was feeling. They were imposingly solid, doors to shut out, not to invite. And as if to prove the point, both entrances had been given a lock, operable from the inside – something that was anomalous in a place where we never felt the need for security, and where the loo door was pulled open and shut on a drawstring.

Though we were given the tour of the new extension, it was clear that this was the last we children could expect to see of it for the rest of the holiday. At the centre of the room was the bed, with the headboard flat against the south wall. It was covered with a soft china-blue and white eiderdown. There was a mirror above, with seashells woven round its top like a head-dress. Pappa and Mamma's cases were stowed, honeymoon-fashion, at the foot, and from this day forth the extension became known among the family as the Honeymoon room.

And yet it did not feel at all romantic. Everything was too convenient, from the double-glazed windows keeping out the draughts, to the blackout blinds promoting later rising. There was something of the ski chalet in the clean pine ceiling beams and walls, the wood not left untreated like the old house. In the east corner, a brand-new Jotul stood on a slate stand, with a neat firewood-and-paper stack and firelighters. A painting of a ship on turbulent seas called *Willing of Jersey* dominated the east wall. A smell that was new and strange hung in the air.

The sleeping area opened on to a small washroom that was perhaps more appealing. It had an air of modest surprise at being the only place on the island where fresh water could be pumped into a basin for shaving, like a real bathroom. And a kettle could be boiled there on a Primus stove for morning tea. Mamma never drank tea, so this had been installed by Pappa with himself in mind. Dordie and I glanced hopefully at a pleasant mezzanine, accessible by stepladder, imagining sleeping there for novelty; but this was to be used for the storage of *dyne* covers, sheets and towels, and there would be no room left to camp.

In the face of so drastic a change, we clung to routine arrival activity as to a life raft. Guests, even family, demanded good behaviour, whatever we might be feeling. Soon Dordie and I were taking Saul and Dinah to choose *lusekofte*. From the window of Mor-mor's room, we could see rubble from the contained explosions to remove a large hump of rock obstructing building work that had been scattered around Bitte Småhølmene – destined, Pappa said, to be covered with turf to form a grassy wilderness. It was bleak and jagged against the smooth granite forms behind. I caught sight of the heron, hunting for shrimp in the shallows by Raspberry Island. It looked like a pirate, standing on peg-legs and craning its cutlass beak towards the water.

The first-night consolations of unpacked cases and supper outside would have taken effect but for the disconcerting sense that we, her cabinet ministers, awaited Mamma's public announcement before deciding whether we liked the Honeymoon quarters or not. It was the idea of having to take a side that was so dreadful. Mamma was very good at meaningful silence – she had always told my sisters that if she did not like a boyfriend they'd know by her omission of praise rather than spoken criticism. And though she congratulated Pappa on keeping it a secret, she did not go on and say that she liked the change. Both were so sensitive and so private.

❈

The summer progressed with vague feelings of discomfort as Dordie showed further independent interests, so that I could not always draw her into every one of my games or laughs. She walked regularly across to a place she called the Beauty Parlour, near Cornwall, on the right arm of the island. There she would lie along a smooth ledge of rock, dipping her feet into a rock pool fed by the sea to let a few strands of seaweed cool and tickle the soft skin of her high arches. I begged to be able to sit there too and, exasperatedly, she allowed me to follow behind her over the rocks and even gave me slimy purifying masks by wrapping the thick seaweed across my face. I slightly distrusted this new Dord and had an awful sense of déjà vu at having to beg for inclusion, as I did anyway with my half-siblings, rather than to expect it as my right. I had always been slightly bossy with her, being naturally more outgoing and strident, though the youngest. But now there was rebellion in the air.

Straight after breakfast, Dordie fetched the two *kaste-sluken* reels from the sail-loft, and she and Saul spent pleasant mornings catching sand crabs, baiting the hooks with leftover bacon rind. I took out my plastic-handled net, but soon gave up to linger by the buckets, count how many they had caught and argue inconsequentially over which seemed likeliest to win in a crab race. The official racecourse was on the Blindleia side and the finishing post was the sea, where the winning crab disappeared in a cloud of sand. The event was given backing music from the gramophone, brought down by Pappa to celebrate a fine evening. I had soon memorised the words to the most-played songs and could sing along, even perform to them. Singing lessons in London had ignited some dramatic ambition and, feeling out of things, I began to show off. 'Oh What a Beautiful Morning' let me air my American accent, and I loved 'Anything You Can Do I Can Do Better', which required two voices. At the opening bars of Charles Trenet's '*L'âme des Poètes*', I cringed and went inside, embarrassed because Pappa always asked Mamma to dance, and she always said no.

I drifted more and more as, together, Saul and Dord claimed Walter Widmer, who at twelve was as competent as we all were hopeless when it came to engines. He arrived one afternoon in a sleek racing boat with crazy stories about the competitive junior racing circuit. He gave Saul, and then Dord, a spin around the islands that fuelled a sort of hero worship in both. Mamma looked a warning at me that a third voyage was too much to ask and so I hung around Sasha, who was reading in the window seat, wearing my Fred Olsen visor and trying to attract her attention. There were prints of famous Napoleonic battles hung on either side of the bay window, the *Bataille de Rivoli*, with foot soldiers on the march, and the *Bataille des Pyramides*, showing a cavalcade brandishing vicious scimitars, and for a while I forgot my isolation in the vividness of these scenes, and in the sight of a handsome old vessel passing along the Blindleia. Dinah, clever and kind, was a sort of natural third and deflected my interruptions of Sasha's reading as only a sensitive guest would bother to do.

On the first weekend of August, Great Uncle Alfred's eighty-fourth birthday was celebrated in style with lobster, cake and champagne. Because the seventh was a Monday, festivities had been pushed back to a Saturday, the day before my own. Old Axel sat in a deckchair and dozed through proceedings wearing a naval blazer and cap, which was pushed askew as his head lolled back gently against the frame. Kay was drinking cherry pop – like Mamma, he never touched alcohol – but turned pink anyway in the long afternoon sun. Pappa stood by his side drinking beer and boasting that he had speared a flounder while snorkelling in the lagoon. It had been an escapade worthy, Aunt Magda said, of James Bond himself. We had all had just a forkful because the flounder was so small, and so rare – fried in brown butter and scattered with parsley, Pappa's culinary *pièce de résistance*.

Over that summer of irreproachable weather, Great Uncle Alfred had recovered much of his bronzed sprightliness and showered his witticisms like confetti over the party, the perfect host. 007 indeed. Helle stalked around like an exotic bird in the brightest caftan with a plate of cocktail mouthfuls. The Småhølmene party had really put their best foot forward. The preparations had taken almost all morning, including Dinah and Saul washing their mother's hair, taking it in turns to pour as Aunt Magda knelt with a beehive of soap-suds over the *brygge*.

The promise of my own birthday celebrations, scheduled for the following day, a Sunday, raised my spirits to such a pitch I didn't mind anything. But though the day dawned as it should – a sunny breakfast table, the saucer of island raspberries picked especially for my consumption, walled round by cards and presents – Mamma and Aunt Magda, in recycled party clothes, set off soon after for a christening party on the mainland. An occasion of this sort very seldom came Mamma's way and she departed, trying hard to contain her excitement.

The hours dragged by without direction or employment for me, left behind, and as the sun crawled over the house I ran painfully across the demolition rubble to where I could keep a lookout for their return. Intermingled with anger that Mamma had deserted me was concern that she might have been caught up in some sort of accident, and so I wallowed in pessimism, reluctant to think I had merely been forgotten about. The final insult when they eventually returned was that they had had a good, even a great, time, so tea and *bløtkake* were sabotaged by my sulk. The culmination of many hidden wounds, I enjoyed seeing it dismantle the party atmosphere. I had felt ignored and overlooked too long and almost relished the disgrace of being sent to my room.

Mamma Goes Solo

T he Kensington townhouse was put on the market at the dawning of the Honeymoon era. A raising bed for a sizeable dependant family, it was no longer needed. The last days there had been curiously impersonal, like living in a shell. I strained my ears to catch the echo of my sisters' lively voices and found that, with them gone, I cared little about the move. I was sorry to leave the garden, which had a beautiful lime tree with plenty of low branches that I could climb. But Pappa was careful to point out that the new garden would be both larger and finer, and that he would build a swing for me from the tallest tree. The contents of home were packed up and what was not bagged for first rental flats or campus accommodation came with us to the new place in the south-west of the country.

When Pappa took us to look around it in the autumn, Dordie and I had spent most of the afternoon on the lawn catching leaves, one for every happy month of the new year. It was a family ritual that, each September, Mamma would take us to the park to stand beneath the London plane trees, waiting for the wind to send a fresh swathe fluttering earthwards. The leaves had a way of evading our clutches, as if swiped by invisible hands. At home we burrowed them away in a drawer as talismans of good fortune. We stuck to the practice superstitiously in our new environment.

The house was gloomy and imposing, surrounded by dense woodland, and Mamma, from the night we moved in, liked to lock her bedroom door at night. Dord and I were to choose bedrooms, one each, which was very grand, but though we kept our belongings separate in a symbolic gesture of independence from one another, we shared my cosier twin-bedded room, sometimes holding hands until we fell asleep. It was undeniably spooky, a place full of dark corners. I was convinced it was haunted, that the silence had ghosts. Only Pappa seemed really happy to be there. He liked space more than the rest of us, and not only the sort of space belonging to long horizons, which the island granted in abundance, but the lofty voids of tall rooms and empty corridors, which the Honeymoon quarters had been a stab at making there.

With the sale came a compounded sense of the value of Småhølmene, its age-old rocks and patterns of nature making any amount of shifting elsewhere appear tolerable. I played a lot of chess at this time and felt that the island was like Mamma's brave queen, the strongest piece on the board, which must be kept in the game at all costs. Over the winter holiday, I challenged whoever I could persuade to sit for half an hour, learning the subtleties of attack and defence, the complexities of '*en passant*' and castling. Chess was the one arena that could hold my attention. I was a butterfly. I wanted to be an astronomer one moment, and an actress the next. I took up the cello, then piano, then singing, dropping each after a short time. My school report was despairing. When I ate, Mamma told me to sit not as if I was about to catch a train, but like a lady. As soon as I had finished my plate I begged to get down, scampering off with a hurried '*Takk for maten*' – Thank you for the food.

The full contingent of siblings was staying for Christmas and, to welcome them, Mamma filled the new house with reassuring, familiar smells, wafting enticingly from the kitchen: orange peel and spices from tree biscuits; nutmeg grated into a white sauce for leeks; the vinegar twang of a court bouillon to poach a huge wild sea trout. We were gathered around the tree in the living-room, when the phone rang with the news that Great Aunt Helle had died. We grieved then – Mamma most acutely of all – at the death of one beloved, one of the final ties to an older world.

This was the last time we would be together as one group, for the following year, my parents split up. Over the spring, long silences that were more dangerous than argument drifted cumulatively around the wider silences of the fortress-like house. Soon everywhere was cloud. Dordie and I, though hardened sleuths when it came to everything improbable, allowed much of reality to pass us by. We filled the quiet with our own laughter and were taken completely by surprise at the announcement of a separation.

One of the great boons of boarding school was that it provided distraction. Mamma bought what she called her 'doll's house' in west London, on a street of old railway workers' houses. She crowded it with lots of familiar things so that almost instantaneously it felt like home. We met Pappa at a French café on Kensington Church Street and he shocked us by giving way to tears. I can never walk past it without thinking of that terrible moment, and the taste of bridge rolls will always remind me of deep sadness. Emmie attempted to rally the troops over the Easter holiday, taking us on endless swimming expeditions to Dolphin Square. She would forget herself lane-swimming while Dord and I larked around like in the old days, pretending to be creatures of the deep. We opened our eyes underwater to feel the chlorine sting and ate Penguin bars in the car on the way home.

Then at half-term Pappa took us to Paris. He had spent his childhood in France and one of his first memories was his mother clamping a chamber pot over his head during air-raids. He remembered squashing chocolate into a warm baguette at breakfast time, a schoolboy's *tartine*, and eating *baba au rhum* walking through the grand avenues of the 16th arrondissement. I begged to be allowed to try all he described so mouth-wateringly. Pappa had conversed in French before he could in English and spoke with no trace of accent. It was a different Pappa I found in Paris. It opened up a window on to his character and struck a balance with the Mor-mor weight of our ancestry as I heard tales of my paternal grandmother, on husband number three when she had taken the boys to live in France, with increasing wonder at having two such formidable forebears.

I drifted away from Pappa and Dord in Galeries Lafayette and had my name called over the tannoy telling me to make my way to the meeting area. I had been secretly looking for a crop-top in the underwear department, embarrassed to announce to Pappa that I felt I was beginning to need one. When we were reunited, he again shed tears of worry and despair. I felt guilty and a little ashamed. But there were many more happy moments. True to his word, Pappa took us to corner bistros for French onion soup, snails and wonderful *steak-frites*. We ate chocolate crêpes from a street vendor and wandered around Montmartre, where Pappa told us stories of the bohemian poets and artists who had lived there. I felt that my eyes were opened, the first time I really engaged with a place outside of Norway or home.

※

The summer proper brought more new scenes. Ten precious days of our holiday were to be spent with family friends at a villa in Corfu, this time with Mamma accompanying. Novelty creates distraction, and Dordie and I found plenty, from the lizards that scuttled up the white stucco buildings, to the breakfasts of thick yoghurt and sweet cake, which the really greedy could spread with sticky fig jam, as I did.

Everywhere was a contrast to the island: the sandy tracks hedged by withered wild plants; the bony cattle grazing off thin grass and the dry heat. We basked in the sea, floating on our backs and looking up at the sky – perhaps not as refreshing as the cold shock of the lagoon, but a pleasant way to pass the time. Late in the evening, when it was cool enough, we ate fish fresh off the boat, with sharp lemons on the sides of our plates to squeeze over.

Mamma had morale boosted by a talkative companion, who had herself been through a messy divorce. I grew tired of her voice. She advised Mamma on a new haircut that made her look more than ever like Ali MacGraw. Groovy new clothes should be purchased in the summer sales when we got back. In place of her wedding ring, Mamma took to wearing an old family heirloom, a gold band with an emerald eye.

The postponement of the trip to Norway could give breathing space, but it could not put off the inevitable. Mamma must face running Småhølmene solo. Emmie was to come for the settling-in stage, at the beginning of a three-week stay. She would be Mamma's right-hand woman, paying special attention to both Dordie and me to distract from Pappa's absence. Fate dealt us a kind hand on the first night on the island. A racing pigeon, blown off course by an almighty storm, landed miserably on the roof of the house. We were enchanted by the unexpected visitor. The following morning Mamma put out milk and breadcrumbs. At first the bird was very shy, but it soon gathered confidence and became quite tame. We were sorry when finally it took wing and flew onwards – it had become a friend – but glad too.

Despite all Emmie's efforts to persuade us into good spirits, it was on this holiday that a new idea dawned: that the island was under threat. We had always fantasised that everyone who saw Småhølmene, including those with neighbouring properties, preferred it to their own homes and were angling to buy it from us. Two millionaire brothers, whose summer houses stood within view, one on the island of Trondarøya, the other opposite us on the mainland, seemed the likeliest to be set on property expansion. In the settlements around us we saw much ostentation, fast boats and bold family crests ripping from the flagpoles, the tallest a staggering eighteen metres tall. Regularly we were startled by the roaring engines of a seaplane taking off, and we ran from the Blindleia side to the top rock to wave as it soared overhead, then had a sinking feeling in the pits of our stomach that it might be taking aerial photographs to show to a prospective buyer.

The sense that we did not have quite what it took to keep up Småhølmene as it deserved was mortifying. It meant that, in our darkest imaginings, the old house was pulled down and in its place something ghastly and modern was erected. The thought started to work its way into our dreams at night. We were all in the old house so there was no concealing it from each other. The scrape of a loosened tile, or the draught whistling through a crack in the windowpanes, broke into our slumber. Morning brought fresh optimism, when, like Alice, we tried imagining six impossible things before breakfast. We thought of the location scouts that would give their eye teeth to shoot a movie on the island, though the field was narrow when it came to stories of lonely rocks and simple living. On the steps of Mor-mor's *Kongeveien*, I found myself wishing for the riches of kings, or at least enough money to give the Hardanger, which was taking on more water than ever, a proper repair job.

For Mamma, there were still a few of the old demons to overcome regarding Småhølmene's management. Cylinders of gas felt heavier in collection, and the question of what to do with the sail-loft now Pappa was gone was too horrendous to deal with. He had not only taken to the sociable side of island life, but brought a wealth of practical know-how, easing the running of the place. At the summer's end, Mamma's entry in the guestbook would contain anxious notes on 'Fridge Gas Changing', 'Pushing Back Procedure' (this begins, 'Get long-handled kitchen broom,' and describes the hazardous-sounding process of repositioning the fridge after changing the lead), and what to do when 'Loo Pump Not Working'.

I traced her actions and feelings eagerly. Her story seemed a continuation of Mor-mor's, who had herself dreaded having to face troublesome, mechanical things without backup, yet was unable to conquer independent impulses. It struck me that even Mamma and Pappa divorcing had in the end harked back to an illustrious record of men being evicted from the island. I scrutinised the photograph of Mor-mor, pinned up among the postcards in the loo. In it, she sits provocatively naked but for a pair of deck shoes, only by careful arrangement of her legs and arms kept within the bounds of decency. Purportedly, Mor-mor had had copies sent to her daughter's fiancés, Simon and then Pappa. The notecards included in the envelope were pure wicked stepmother: 'Before you choose the chicken, look at the old hen.' And it had really come to pass. As she had booted off Beste Pappa to make way for Lars, so husbands of the next generation, Mamma's husbands, had been exiled from Småhølmene in turn.

As the days wore on, I tried to be especially conscientious in the hope of easing the load. I learnt to use the outboard motor and enjoyed having the freedom of the sea that it gave. It also brought a sense of usefulness, for when Mamma was reluctant to drive into town to buy provisions, I took the helm instead. The way to map a safe course past the many underwater rocks was to draw imaginary alignments between points, like a dot-to-dot drawing. I memorised hard and soon reaped the benefits. Mamma knew I could be trusted alone when I anticipated her before she spoke a command. After ten days, the Gladstone family arrived on the Kristiansand flight and passed Emmie at the airport on her return journey. I drove the boat to Bliksund to pick them up and waved triumphantly before easing into dock.

Mamma remained happily in Mor-mor's old bedroom, with the excuse that it left the Honeymoon room free for Isla and Clova's mother, Nicola, who was new to the island. Sleeping there, she would escape the creaking floorboards and shutting of doors, which were the accompaniment to night-times in the old house. Isla, Clova, Dordie and I crammed into the dorm, which suited our designs for midnight-feasting and ghost stories. They remembered the all-important safety concerns of the island, to be careful on the rainy rocks and to pinch the last spark from a candle-wick before retiring for the night.

I was the one most prone to getting into scrapes. I was short-sighted when it came to spotting jellyfish, trapped my fingers in door hinges and bumped my head sitting up in the night. Mamma teased that the island medical supplies were for my sole use. An overflowing wicker basket spilled rolls of plaster, cans of insect repellent and tubes of ointment for burns, cuts and grazes. The worst calamity was soon forgotten with one or two arnica pills dissolved under the tongue. Mamma had a first-aid certificate from London and an outdated medical compendium that fell open on a page with a graphic illustration of an emergency birth, which appalled and secretly fascinated Dordie and me.

On the right arm of the island, a little way from the boathouse, a ravine about one metre wide and two deep bisects a flat plateau of rock. This posed an irresistible challenge. I looked down on Isla, Dordie and Clova milling around by the water's edge inspecting Dord's Beauty

Parlour and decided to circumvent them with an impressive leap. But, misjudging the distance, I fell and cracked my head on landing. Their worried faces danced before my eyes as I came to. Asking groggily whether my white jeans had been stained, I raised a hand to my forehead and felt a warm clot of blood. It was actually very minor but caused further drama. A budding hypochondriac, for days after I could not prevent myself running my hand over the egg left behind.

Lurking behind every minor accident there was the spectre of something more serious. What if I had to be airlifted to hospital? Would a boat arrive in time? Etc., etc. A sense of powerlessness gave rise to ghastly fears. Mamma was a mine of terrible stories, telling of fires and drownings. The sea was fickle, quiet as a millpond one moment, raging the next. Superstitions attached to it were to be respected. '*Havet gir, havet tar*' – 'The sea giveth, the sea taketh away' – was a widow's lament. If one of us knocked our glass with a knife or fork over supper, Mamma put her hand out to stop the high metallic ring, in case a sailor should be drowned at sea.

Then one morning, Nicola and Mamma ventured off on a Ladies Only expedition to Lillesand, on the hunt for knitting patterns. We watched them go, waving from the wilderness at the furthest point of the left arm of the island. Heather like a thick Persian carpet rolled out along the rock. It is the national flower of Norway. On the mainland, roaming willow ptarmigan grow plump from young plants before being shot when they are full of heathery flavour. On the island it provides some welcome colour and attracts bumblebees. *Lyng* honey is amber-coloured and very thick. There is always a pot at Småhølmene, kept high to save it from ants.

We climbed down to the angelica bushes to inspect the green caterpillars, stooping when our eyes fell on a raspberry. The fruit tasted piercingly sweet, and cool from the overshadowing boulders. In the shallow channel below we knew we would find water snails. We jumped down to hunt out those with striped shells and the pointy, white-tipped variety. The channel narrowed beneath the Japanese Bridge. Strips of sea showed through the slat-panelled walkway as the stream widened again in the Little Bay, from where, leaving our clothes on the rocks, we swam bravely out towards the bathing steps, at the other end of the lagoon.

The sun climbed over the house and still there was no sign of the knitting party. We kept stout-hearted and sanguine, making an adequate lunch out of rather stale cinnamon buns, which we had sitting on the rocks where we could keep a lookout for the boat. But as the afternoon crept onwards we were led on to wonder, to doubt and finally to despair. We were huddled in an emergency summit meeting to discuss possible action when a sailing schooner with folded rigging appeared carrying Mamma and Nicola as its cargo. The *Lego Boat* was being towed behind and soon both vessels were moored safely on the *brygge*. They had run out of fuel on the approach into Lillesand and floated aimlessly on the currents before managing to flag down help. The rescuing party was invited to tea and somehow Mamma managed to make what remained of a cherry cake stretch for us all to have a very little piece. She glowed with pride as they admired first the neat contrivances of the house, then the picturesque view over the Blindleia, along which they planned to sail all the way to Kristiansand. By the time they left, our spirits had much improved.

When the moon was rising, Mamma took us out in the Hardanger, daring total waterlogging. She rowed around the island slowly, so we could marvel at the changes brought about by the darkness. The rocks seemed huge, patched with light and shadow like a charcoal drawing. Strips of cloud glowed white in the twilit sky. The heron took wing as we passed Raspberry Island and we heard its heavy wing-beats as it passed the boat.

The following day we set off to swim in flotilla forma-tion around the island. Dord was in the vanguard and as leader had mask and snorkel, keeping watch for jellyfish. Swimming in tandem at the rear were Clova and I, with Isla in the middle, a pile of blonde hair and long lily-stem neck emerging from the water. We crossed to the mouth of the lagoon, where the encouraging shouts of Mamma and Nicola, sunning themselves by the boathouse, made us turn to give a parting wave before being carried along the currents of Gull Channel. Dord did an admirable job, keeping at bay any fears she had, swimming back when she outstripped us and, when she saw a jelly, saying with wonderful cool that it would perhaps be best if we kept in line behind her. A leader who panicked could alarm the rest of the party, leading to an aborted mission at the Velvet Steps. It was considered rather poor form to get out there, nearing halfway, but taking a breather to jump from the high point was allowable. We pulled ourselves up on the slippery rocks while the wind pricked our skin with goose-bumps. Then we held our noses and splashed in again one after another, feeling the delicious fizz of the bubbles on impact.

The shallows at the back of the house, where the fisherman set his eel traps, were by far the most unpleasant stretch of the circuit. The water plants tickled our stomachs and thick sheaves of dislodged weed bobbed past on the surface. From there, along the right arm of the island, visibility was good and swimming was again a pleasure. A steep sea-shelf meant that the water was an almost tropical blue and at any moment, it seemed, exotic fishes would start swimming around us. We slowed down to admire the rocks, sometimes marbled, at others white as alabaster. Seen at a distance it was one of the most beautiful parts of Småhølmene.

We had only to turn back into the lagoon to complete our swim, when we heard a shout coming from the boathouse. Mamma and Nicola were kneeling over the *brygge* and looking intently at the water. The family ring, which was loose on her finger, had slipped off before Mamma could stop it. It had pinballed down the thick weed to the seabed and was lost from sight. Sand clouds had risen, lowering visibility, at the first frantic scrabbling. Before we could begin to join the hunt we had to wait for the water to settle, and I ran to fetch goggles from the sail-loft.

We spent so long diving for the ring, without success, that we were very wrinkled and cold when we got out of the water. Mamma was shell-shocked. She stirred a great pot of chocolate to revive both spirit and body. When her friends Roland and Marianne arrived unexpectedly with all four children in tow, and the eldest two showed willing to try their luck finding the ring, we were persuaded back into the water with hope renewed.

There is an old English folktale, *The Fish and the Ring*, telling the story of a peasant girl whose fate it is to marry a nobleman's son. The nobleman, who has the ability to divine the future, tries to have the infant child drowned. But the tiny bundle is discovered by a fisherman and he brings the girl up as his daughter. When the son, riding past the fisherman's cottage, sees the girl, he falls in love with her. But the proud father still opposes the match. He tries to force the girl over a cliff but she wrestles herself to safety. Exasperated, he takes a ring from his finger and throws it into the sea, saying that when the girl finds the ring, she and his son can wed. Then one day, as she prepares a great fish to be served at a state banquet, she finds the ring inside the creature's stomach. She slips it on her finger and when she is serving the guests at table, the nobleman sees the ring and, submitting to inexorable fate, allows the young couple to marry.

For the rest of the holiday, when we caught a fish, we removed the innards carefully, slicing open the stomach and really expecting to see Mamma's gleaming gold-and-emerald band. Were we to find it, she might then marry a prince, or nobleman. But there was only sand, or fry, or baby crabs.

❊

Great Uncle Alfred died five years after Helle, in 1996. I had grown very fond of him. A mischief-maker himself, he took pleasure in having young tearaways around him. He made the most marvellous 'snouffling' noises, with a range of meaning taking one from approval, to affection, to gentle chastisement. These sounds were reserved especially for best dogs and children. He had been walking proof of the adage that what you liked must be good for you. He breakfasted off boiled eggs seasoned with dashes of Worcestershire Sauce and demanded steak suppers, though the Norwegian au pair (a live-in carer who fought valiantly to keep Alfred's behaviour in check) warned of the toxicity of red meat. He drank like a fish and washed down heavy meals with medicinal swigs of Kümmel.

Generously, Alfred had left each great niece and nephew a sum of money in his will to put towards education and travel, and his daughters – Mamma's cousins – invited us to Chelsea Square to choose a keepsake to remember him by. I struggled to fix on an object and was guided by Dordie on what to choose: a prancing white china poodle, which I placed among other treasured objects, displayed on the chest of drawers in my bedroom. The house was sold shortly after, so that Shyllevigen alone stood as witness to the communion between the two families.

Christmases thereafter would be hosted by Aunt Anne in Cheshire, our family's arrival filling her home with noise and women. It was an archetypical Georgian English country house, lived in by Uncle Richard's family for many generations, but our celebrations fell firmly into the Scandinavian mould. Aunt Anne worked hard to make things as Mor-mor would have liked. The kitchen smelled of dill, spice and sugar. I could sit quietly at the scrubbed table for hours, watching her poach large salmon in the fish kettle, stirring sauces and checking on pastry that was baking blind. When it had cooled, I was allowed to fill the golden cases with delicious soft onions and bacon, or string beans bagged and frozen after the summer glut. These would form the mainstay of warming winter lunches. She let me whip cream for the Christmas 'peasant girl', the nursery pudding of cooking apple sweetened with brown sugar and rum and crispy breadcrumbs, or make icing for the pepper biscuits. I piled the table with coloured sheets of paper from which to weave heart-shaped baskets for the tree in the hall. Marzipan was hidden inside each on the night before Christmas and, last thing before bed, a bowl of porridge left out for the *julenisser*, the Christmas elf. When the banqueting began, there was some English fare on offer, such as mince pies and even a plum pudding, but the Norwegian sweets won out with us, willing to let things and customs Scandinavian hold sway whenever possible.

True independence came late for Mamma. Having children soon after she married, she had given much of her working life to raising a family, excepting a short stint at Christie's auction house on her return from Australia. After the divorce, she took a job serving lunches at a London day school. She soon moved up the ranks to become a teaching assistant, helping the younger pupils with reading. She had always been passionate about children's books and found fulfilment in her work. We were all proud of her, and learnt to share the well-loved Mrs Seymour with a sense of privilege.

Dordie climbed successfully through the forms at secondary school to become head girl and a star pupil. Using Great Uncle Alfred's funds, she went to Botswana for her year out, and when she returned in time for the summer holiday in Norway I felt she was a stranger to me. Her experiences refreshed the interest of the older girls, however, with whom she had suddenly much more in common than me. She and Sasha spent most of the day in deep conference, set apart from the rest of us. I did not even try to join in, sensing that my presence would contribute nothing. Instead I tried to appropriate any visitor, valuing especially the comings and goings of boyfriends, whom I never judged critically, so that it was always a surprise when a relationship failed. I was a pet whose company was sought as recourse, never simply for its own sake. I was obsessed with growing up quickly, to bring myself to a level with the others, in danger of learning too late the importance of touching each base in life.

Pappa's one-time presence on the island had become like the visions of a dream. Concrete proof lay in the Honeymoon room, however, which was, as he had envisaged it for Mamma and himself, a place of sanctuary for couples seeking a degree of separation from the party in the old house. I entered gladly now, sprawling across the soft china-blue and white eiderdown with my nose in a book, or sitting propped against the wall in a sun stripe, a sketchpad on my knee, before a still life of island flowers, dried-out crab claws and dark strips of popping weed. I loved the one-to-ones it allowed. It was as though being there raised all conversational embargoes, facilitating free discourse and expression. With no one to overhear, grievances were aired and lightened in the telling, and alliances formed. It was quite as good as the rocks themselves for secret summits.

The Primus stove in the washroom for early morning tea was out of service and the fresh-water pump too had become defunct, so that the principles of Honeymoon existence were in many respects the same as for the rest of the island. Yet there were elements that made it special and different. The tang of new wood had faded and now the smell felt like what it would be to sit in a pine forest after rain. When it was actually raining, the Jotul stove meant that the occupants could stay put, warm, dry and comfortable, thus easing the load in the sitting-room. And, arched over by wild scarlet rugosa roses, the slate pathway running from the *brygge* to the east-facing door had a magic effect, like the entrance to an enchanted castle; indeed, in turn, each sister emerged from beneath the bowers with a husband on her arm, ready to live happily ever after.

It appears to me now as though all the older girls fell in love, became engaged and married, at precisely the same moment; and that just as Dord was beginning to draw level with them in my mind, she again slipped behind as first Sasha, then Becky and Emmie entered this new stage in life. I felt that their becoming wives reduced my claim as sister, and was careful what demands I made of them.

The weddings themselves, though at different times of year, and all in London, took place with some Norwegian feeling. I made Sasha a wedding banquet of spinach soup with Dagmar's buttery egg-boats, poached wild sea trout and new potatoes, cucumber salad and herby mayonnaise – the best of Scandinavian summer cooking. It was not real island cooking, rather it was celebration food, associated in my mind with Christmas or Easter or 17 May, Norwegian Constitution Day. Blueberries and raspberries with heavy cream, the three colours of the Norwegian flag, was my tribute pudding. Heady with success, I promised Becky a *Kransekake* for the big day, and mortifyingly had to withdraw my offer as trials shrank, or broke apart. It was a costly experiment, requiring kilograms of almonds which all ended up binned. Peter Widmer arrived in London with Norwegian flags, little coloured parasols and shiny crackers to decorate the cake, but in the end, I hid the box in shame. The stand-in, dark chocolate cake (shop-bought), had real rose petals on top and needed no further adornment. Becky chided me for my overambition and I vowed to master the skill in the end.

It was either the wrong time of year for a Norwegian honeymoon, or my sisters knew that island life was no rest cure. Besides, Småhølmene seemed to have had an ill effect on marriages. Superstition was beginning to cling around the place though we would never admit to it. Mor-mor's *affaires*, so numerous and so public, were a legacy that must be renounced, and that was only easy to accomplish outside the realm where it was impossible to escape her. The island might remove all impediments to true love at the start, but that love then had a tendency to crumble in the shadows of the rocks, and rust at the touch of the salty sea. It was no accident that boyfriends were tested there, but a honeymoon was not a time for tests.

Brothers-in-law

Perhaps it was the arrival of the millennium that finally nudged the family into some modest modernising. The autumn of 2000 saw the installation of a second washroom, tucked away at the far end of the inner part of the boathouse. It was to possess many luxurious features. There was to be electrically heated water and electric lighting, a cut away from the oil and Tilley lamps that we made do with, even loved, in the old house; a sink and a shower with hot and cold running water; under-floor heating operated by a little dial in the wall, to take some of the chill from the floor tiles first thing. It was envisioned as an enclave of clean comfort, partitioned away from the rest of the grime.

Norwegian architecture often seemed to have an almost symbiotic relationship with nature. Wood was built into rock with merged endings designed to create optical illusions of seamless evolution. The boathouse exhibited this magnificently with its hoists and slipways running into the lagoon, and the front part exposed to the winds where the boats were stored over the winter. The contrast between that and this new inner sanctum – where the only concession to what was outside was a tiny window looking out on to rock, saffron-speckled lichen and just a peep of sky in the top-right corner – was striking indeed.

Following the installation of a laundry machine even the Norwegian *kofte* were as new, given a facelift by a marvellous Norwegian detergent for woollens. Black-and-white cardigans and jumpers were cat's-eye clean, luminous even in darkness. Washing-up became easier. Wearing head torches if there was no moon, we made our way carefully past the Troll's Saucepan to the boathouse, to fill a bucket with hot water and suds. This saved time and gas, for the stove no longer need be used to heat the pail. Island life became easier and we were rewarded for embracing change.

There was one aspect of the bathroom of which I could not approve. Though it was inconsistent of me to use some, and not other, conveniences, I found the idea of a shower at Småhølmene went against every principle. The salty lagoon was unmatched for smoothing the skin and relaxing the muscles. We had spent our early childhood summers in a state best described as clean enough, which remained enough for me. Now island guests drifted towards the boat-house as if drawn by a magnet, with towels over their arms and clean clothes, to wash and dress for the day or evening – somehow one always had to dress after. I felt they lost out by denying themselves the elemental joy of being a little salty, which encapsulated the holiday feeling for me, and I refused to use the shower, however sorely I was tempted on wet days, or the days when a chill took hold.

There was no going back once we got used to the small luxuries of such a room. But with it came new expenses. For a private island, the management of Småhølmene had incurred amazingly few hidden costs hitherto; our habits were frugal, the summer was generous in its supplies of light and heat, and the sea and land abundant in their harvests. An island kitty was suggested, which had all the financial clout of a piggy bank as we faced an influx of staggeringly high water and electricity bills.

✳

The year before I left school, a curious incident took place on the island. Carrying a saw over the rocks to cut away a wilderness of dead juniper, Mamma took a bad tumble. I had been watching her and, the moment before she fell, was struck forcibly by what I perceived to be her similarity to Mor-mor, with that disregard for her own safety, which seemed wilfully to court accident. I flinched before her footing went off, as one anticipates dropping a glass before it slips through one's fingers and shatters on the floor. Though not badly hurt, she was shaken by the fall. Her visits to the island dwindled, and then with the surprise announcement that she would no longer be spending her summers in Norway, stopped altogether.

Mamma was fifty-three when she was diagnosed with Parkinson's disease. She had been having difficulty swinging her arms while walking. She began to limp, at first almost imperceptibly, and then more noticeably. The evidence mounted up and the doctor gave sentence.

It takes time to understand and come to terms with illness. The thing about Parkinson's is that it worsens at the first sign of stress. Anxiety is given physical articulation: in early onset a faint tremor; as the disease advances, motor dysfunction that can immobilise the body. To accomplish the same ends, a Parkinson's patient must invest five times the effort of a healthy person. Mamma fought valiantly and overcame much. But the island put a heavy tax on the frail. It was always a place that needed two hands and a strong body to navigate.

One effect the diagnosis had on my mother was for the first time to question the long-term future of Småhølmene in our family. The island was her nest egg. She talked of putting it on the property market and it took all our united powers of dissuasion to stop her. We children went as much as we could, lavished attention on it and directed our energy towards making her believe it to be worth keeping. We returned to England, hoping to pique her interest with stories of the gulls and eider ducks, how the water had been warm or cold, or the day-trippers who had been successfully scared off with Mor-mor-inspired displays of nudity. She smiled fondly as if we were talking about a lost world, perhaps divining that the crucial balance would remain missing while she, Mamma, was absent. There would be disagreements and infighting about the fairness of opposing a sale when it was hers to sell. Tension would run high.

The sense of being under a time sentence brightened all the colours, injecting island life with an almost shocking vividness. Luckily my new brothers-in-law normalised things when all grew too intense and fanciful. They diffused atmospheres and led by uniformly good cheer. One showed a passion for fishing, and came with rods and tackle, as though our old reels had had their day. Another liked exercise, so that there were two brand-new red kayaks for fitness expeditions. And the third loved food.

❊

The Småhølmene kitchen posed challenges to the gastronomically adventurous. It was badly equipped for a start. The temperature of the oven was impossible to control. Once ignited, the flame sped around what looked like the track of model train, so that a complete rectangle of bright blue-and-yellow blazed up in a hiss of gas. Cooking required some wizardry to make a dish come off. But Alexander, Emmie's husband, was not one to be easily deterred. He chucked away the spices that were past their use-by date, replacing them with little containers of saffron, paprika and dill seed among other things, and brought a giant tin of good quality olive oil to last a whole summer. A large paella pan arrived. It fitted over the barbecue, making rice-and-fish a staple of gramophone evenings. Colourful sacks of Calasparra rice and dried sweet peppers were interlopers in the island store cupboard.

I watched Al cook and felt sure that, while I had an interest in food, I should never reach the same level of accomplishment and exactitude. Like Pappa, Al believed it was worth going the extra mile, rather than simply making do, or cutting corners. With an ingeniously stocked larder he overcame the severest of the island kitchen's limitations, reformed our tastes and radically transformed the way we ate.

While British gastronomy was in a state of constant flux, swayed by every influence, the food of Scandinavia remained stalwartly the same. Cold meats and fish formed the mainstay of the summer diet. Potatoes and dark grains gave substance to a meal, with refreshment by way of a cucumber salad, or ripe tomatoes. It was food that was solid, clean and plain, a sober matron disapproving of the frippery of southern Europe. But it had secret flashes of ornamentation. I loved its sour and pickled elements. With preserved elderberries, the woodiness of beetroot was eliminated and it became something complex and remarkable. Tart currants made any pudding seem grand with their rich glossy pigments. Fluffy white goat's cheese sang of the mountains, as though exhaling some of the pure air, breathing sweet grass and clover.

Norwegian food could also seem retro, with its self-consciously decorative sprigs of curly parsley and mayonnaise piping. Even the packaging sang of a bygone era, so that going to the supermarket had the allure of a museum visit. Norwegian eggs continued to lay pristine white. Sweet pastries all had snow flurries of nibbed sugar. There was honesty and simplicity in the pleasures this afforded, and I relished the sameness. It was part of what it meant to be connected, and I clung to it as a fond memory. But the way we cooked on the island had always been something rather different. We were building our own culinary histories, with Mor-mor as the starting point, so that the ritual making of certain of her dishes became part of every summer. Al, however, added a whole new dimension.

As for drink, ice-cold beer was thought an elixir over meals of grilled shellfish. I pretended to like it more than I did, mostly to keep abreast with my brother and sisters. There was something about the bitter hoppy taste that made me shudder a little with every swig. I tried to control the movement, but Dord caught me once and said, 'I don't know why you drink it, you don't like it.' My tastes were like Mamma's, rather childish. I shied away from anything untried and hadn't learnt much to enjoy any alcohol. When the Velvet Steps were temporarily dubbed the Vodka Steps I felt almost aggrieved. Emmie and Becky had shots of ice-cold liquor during a midnight sauna, while a group of their friends were staying. It was an intoxicating mix. A game of truth-or-dare followed, resulting in a mass exodus to the Velvets, where, in the moonlight, they leapt naked one by one into the water. The element of danger – the hidden rocks that had to be avoided with a run and spring – cemented this as one of the great events of a generation.

❋

That each one of us would develop entirely distinct and sometimes conflicting ways of being on the island was to be expected. If the island made each one of us more like ourselves, then it followed that, as characters became more firm and resolute in adulthood, it would become more difficult for us to cohabit peaceably. It was like having five queen bees, and no workers. (Thomas was impossible to draw into argument and the brothers-in-law also held their peace, so that the real wrangling took place between us women.) Directions crossed in the air. Authority was asserted, contested and then retracted. We learnt to hope never to be with Emmie on a wet day on the island, as she took bad weather as a personal affront against herself. Indeed the claustrophobic feeling of a rainy Småhølmene day in childhood widened with the passing years into a sense of the island's not really being big enough for us all, not in one go anyway. Dordie was the one oftenest in a position of neutrality during any argument. She was someone to be won over for an outright victory, the all-important casting vote to make three against two.

Our connection was still strong, at times even psychic. We could anticipate what the other was going to say and often finished sentences for each other. Brought closer by the divorce, we shared the excitements as well as the scars of growing up: crushes, first boyfriends, heartbreak. I felt no one deserved Dord. At Småhølmene, any sweetheart was given the sister vetting, and not only by me. If the Honeymoon room was taken – and because seniority dictated who slept there, it often was – the sail-loft was the next best thing for privacy. There, camping mattresses were kept for when extra beds were needed. It quickly became cosy with night lights perched on the trunks and window-sills, and a milk jug of anemones by the bed. When it was taken, the rest of the party tried to block their ears to the sound of murmurs drifting along the connecting attic. But we all united when it came to a sister's – or brother's – happiness. We were very pro-romance: an unusual outcome for a family acquainted with divorce.

Mamma's romanticism suffered no abatement. When we had walked past a flower stall as children, she would whisper what it would be for a lover to buy the whole thing for her, and not just a single bouquet. We were taught to throw apple skin over our shoulders to divine, from the shape it formed on landing, the first letter of the name of the person we would marry. Her romantic ambition was lofty and perhaps unrealistic. She herself dated the pinnacle of her romantic experience to a five-hour-long chance encounter on the deck of the *Canberra* while in port in Colombo. I had similar yearnings for instant attraction, overwhelming feeling and devotion. Småhølmene was the backdrop for my most ardent imaginings. Both spiritually and physically, it was the great gift I could give to someone.

Through university I had boyfriends, though none was especially serious. At any show of fickleness, Mamma warned, 'You must not become like Olga or Angela.' Angela was my father's mother and married no fewer than four times, besides numerous affairs. She had not been able to resist a conquest any more than my Norwegian grand-mother. The idea that I might have inherited tendencies towards flightiness, from either side, was unappealing and I hoped unlikely, as a future rose before me in which no man satisfied. At moments, Mamma also held herself up as example of the pitfalls of an excess of sensibility, of too romantic a disposition, something that flummoxed me because I felt it was an unfair representation of herself and events: she had been unlucky, not impossible.

For the first time in my life, I missed a Småhølmene summer while living in Paris. The option of a year abroad counting towards a four-year degree programme, even though I would be studying literature among students for whom English was a second language, was irresistible. I took a back seat in class and read books I liked rather than those prescribed, and haunted cafés and bars, markets and bookshops rather than devoting hours to the library. I had my own flat, barely furnished, with a view over a bamboo garden and the laundrette on the rue Bichat. I bought an old art-school table from the market, uneven with paint and the chiselled initials of pupils. Three days a week I took a job working as a pastry chef. The kitchen window looked on to a bustling street market and we played the BBC World Service as we made the day's cakes and buns. I felt Mor-mor's disciple, exploring the deep, glamorous world of the French capital.

Preparing to leave, I anticipated heartbreak. In homage to Paris I cut my hair into a gamine French bob and packed the few new clothes I had bought with my earnings carefully in my suitcase. The autumn after I returned to finish my degree, thinking I would never get over leaving the city, I fell madly in love.

It was the start of my last winter term at university, and Trinity's squares were touched with amber and red. On a blustery night, I was hurrying across the road on a green man when someone vaguely familiar passed me. We both turned to glance back, smiling from the safety of our opposite pavements. He was tall and slim, with an unruly mop of dark curly hair. He had a dishevelled, academic look, like a young don. He wore glasses in the library but never outside of studying, having what he called 'aesthetic pretensions' that meant he always cut a dash with his caps and waistcoats and sometimes a flower in his buttonhole. We had not really spoken but the next time I saw him, feeling surprisingly self-assured, I invited him to my campus rooms where, low on stocks, we chomped on early russet apples and drank tea.

His name was Patrick, known by all as Paddy. He was born on the autumn equinox, the youngest of five siblings. This formed an incidental bond between us, and I heard echoed in the characters he painted, my own propensity to lionise my family. The Bresnihans come from County Mayo, but Paddy's mother's side of the family hail from Sligo, Yeats's country. This place dominated his talk and I listened rapt to the stories of his childhood; the summer sailing school at Rosses Point, and the walks in Hazel Wood, like in the great poem, 'The Song of Wandering Aengus'. The place names alone sounded so romantic – Streedagh, Coole and Lissadell – I longed to visit. In turn, I told him of the island. I drew a map so he would understand the layout. 'You would love it,' I said. Only as I heard the words did I realise that I felt completely confident of their truth.

We became inseparable. He hid presents for me around the campus, window ledge or flowerpot revealing a small packet of dried Turkish figs, or a delicious bar of chocolate. The university became a map of our romance. He slipped fragments of poems and novels through my letter box. I tried to keep up, showing Paddy my favourite haunts along the canal or in Dublin's great squares, initiating him into certain elements of the Nordic diet, starting with smoked cod's roe, which I spread on to lavishly buttered hot toast with a grind of pepper and fresh spritz of lemon juice. It was a delicious elevenses, or garden lunch, with the addition of a fennel salad and green soup. This was the sort of snack-meal he would say reminded him of his mother, who had sadly died while he was in his first year at university. I loved the stories he told me of Jeanette. I felt sure we would have liked each other. I revered any couple who had weathered the course and always felt Paddy's parents' story to be a real love story. It was one of his gifts to me, letting me share it through his tales.

We could at times be as much like brother and sister as girlfriend and boyfriend. I was almost two years older and often took the lead in our relationship, but this would shift in the moments I felt fragile or depressed. We both got mumps in the run-up to finals, first Paddy and then me. I got it far worse and had to be quarantined. It hurt to laugh and to eat. Paddy looked at me carefully and sympathetically as tears came to my eyes trying to take a bite of food. I sat my exams in solitary confinement and when I came out of the last paper, he was waiting with an enormous bunch of flowers.

There was no question of our breaking up at the end of our time at Trinity. In the days before I left Ireland we planned our next move. Paddy's best friend George and I had driven down to Rosses Point in his battered-up old Volkswagen. The journey was slow as the car lumbered along the windy coastal road, weighed down with trunks of books and clothes. Paddy met us at Austies pub, one of his favourite watering holes, with a view over Sligo Bay. All three of us were bursting full of hope and idealism for the future. We would move to London, find work and save to get a place of our own. The fact that we would be living in Mamma's basement did little to dampen the grandness of our vision.

❋

In 2005 the south of Norway basked under a heatwave. The sea was low, revealing rocks bleached with dry salt and barnacles parched like mini Etnas. Even the seagulls were quiet, as though stunned by the sweltering weather.

When Paddy visited Småhølmene in July, wanting to hold up for admiration my hardy, island self, I took him on arrival straight to the Velvet Steps for a dive and a swim. We flung our cases on the bed and raced off across the baking rocks, scorching the soles of our feet. Ambitiously we set out to swim right the way round the left arm and back through the lagoon. Settling into a rhythm, Paddy told me the story of O'Dowd, the chieftain of Tireragh, who fell in love with a mermaid. O'Dowd stole her magic mantle while she slept so that she would become human and they could marry. Years later, after she had borne seven children, Nemain recovered her mantle, which her husband had hidden. She turned each child to stone and disappeared beneath the waves. With Paddy there was a story to accompany every mood or action, and right then he was O'Dowd, and I was Nemain. We returned to the little wild shrubbery to pick sea samphire. It tasted salty and clean eaten straight from the root. We collected a bucketful and boiled it for supper, melting butter over it and sprinkling extra salt.

Each morning, not bothering to dress, we slipped from bed, made our way downstairs and jumped straight into the sea. We breakfasted late on boiled eggs, bread and black coffee. Over the long afternoons Paddy rowed us to an island for a picnic, often to Raspberry, though sometimes we went further afield exploring the inlets around Calvøya. On the return journeys we caught many mackerel, which seemed stupefied by the warmth of the water. Soon we were both chestnut brown.

Døgnvild – *døgn* a twenty-four-hour period, and *vild* meaning wild – describes the disorientation of time induced by poor sleep in turn brought on by the short nights or rather twilights. It is common among islanders, especially in the north. The 'wild twenty-four hours' makes time stretch like elastic. It can make a week seem an extension of a single day, filtering nights into day and dream into reality. Our sleep at Småhølmene was wild. Staying up late into the night, talking about the future, Paddy and I slept fitfully as dawn peeped through the curtains. We became accustomed to, and enjoyed, this curious new tiredness. The delirium of time became part of a heightened consciousness, all part of the island's spell.

When we returned to our separate summer plans, the end of July and then August dragged interminably. While I took part-time work in London, Paddy went back to Sligo to await the results of his finals with his family. He sent me letters every other day, hammered out on his battered Olympia typewriter. They were full of romance and longing: real old-fashioned love letters. Writing provided him not only with mental but also physical escape. The walk to the post office on the sea front and back again was his daily exercise. Life at Rosses Point was not so different from Småhølmene. There was a small sailing dinghy with a red cabin he had his eye on, the focus of his dreams and schemes, alongside me. He addressed me as 'his Titan other' and used the private terminology of our relationship: 'inextricating' to describe our physical and spiritual union; 'second break-fasts', which had been an important ritual of our life together at university, an excuse for an early meeting in the day, taken invariably on the stoop in front of our campus rooms. He quoted masses of poetry and told me the books he was reading and the ideas he garnered from them. Paddy was an idealist and a thinker. In one letter he wrote of himself as 'a prospective romantic' and he loved me with all the courage and belief I could ask.

The times I had been less sure had put him in a cold rage. Doubt to him was like a weed in a beautiful garden. His grandiloquent passion never allowed for half measures. It was in my genetic make-up to second-guess, and to look for problems. It was by being in love myself that I discovered the ways in which the divorce history had made me not only less able to trust another person, but less able to trust my feelings for them. When we were together, all niggling worry disappeared. Apart, I combed through each agonised telephone call and tried to divine meanings from the frayed threads. I needed his belief in us to anchor my own.

We both did well in our exams. Neither of us had felt really nervous. Paddy had great confidence in his abilities and I had stopped caring. It became even more important for us to believe in the world we could create together. We were expected to make something of ourselves, use our good grades for the greater good. I could feel Paddy roll his eyes as he described conversations with his father discussing his future over endless bottles of wine. Hangovers always made him painfully depressed and he began to suffer by being away from me too long. No one understood except us, he said. He prophesied our being 'together for as far as one can see'. 'There is so much to look forward to,' he wrote in his penultimate letter, when September had come at last.

PART III

WINTER

Note for the plane

Darling Till,

I am attempting to put myself into my contrary mother's mind, thus possibly enabling me to illustrate her reaction to your crazy Robinson Crusoe plan to live on Småhølmene this coming winter with Paddy. Whatever her feelings would have been, they would essentially have come out as dramatically pro or blackly anti, there would have been nothing in between. I believe, even though she would never have thought to do it herself, that she would have been amused by the romance of the adventure. She would, of course, mention such salient points as the summer-built structure of the little place and the possibility of being iced in with no running water, no working loo and maybe the close company of a mink family, nesting in the old Maples sofa and leaving a horrid acrid stench in the air.

Mor-mor was the creator of what has become our family summer paradise. It is entirely her spiritual gift to us all and anyone who came and understood it as she did was always welcomed. But in her unpredictable way she turned pretty horrid if some visiting summer guest forgot to parsley the French butter dishes or made the ghastly mistake of addressing her as 'Mor-mor' to her face. 'Don't call me that, it is so non-U.' Yes, she was a devout Nancy Mitford follower.

On the subject of you two being essentially locked up together in what I imagine to be chilly discomfort, I can only say *bonne chance*. I should hate to be cold and damp and to be overcome by cabin fever whilst marooned by the winter Skagerrak storms. But maybe you will monitor the wildlife, the ducks and various gulls overwintering there.

Promise to wear life jackets – the sea is a killer in a very short space of time in winter. I know how casual you have been about bicycle safety; do not be the same in Norway. You see, Dort 5, I should be so sad to lose you. I know there is safety in numbers but every one of you is equally valuable to me.

I salute your bravado and wish you both a 'Calm Sea and Prosperous Voyage'. Mamma

A Winter Plan Offers a Solution

The time was ripe for a change in thinking about Småhølmene. Its underuse, three months out of twelve, argued in favour of Mamma's letting the island go. She had held off thus far, knowing it would break our hearts, but I wanted her to keep it for herself, not for us. I sought out ways in which I could make her value the island anew, without necessarily going there herself. A long, meaningful stay, building ties with the mainland, was one possibility. Mor-mor's best letters had always come in September, when she remained on the island rather than returning to Oslo with the rest. They were filled with description and some inspirational flourishes, awakening all Mamma's sympathies and shared sensibilities. The quieter season had definite virtues, though they were of a more modest and discreet variety. But all this was distant history. We evacuated at the end of August, just as the boat traffic along the Blindleia was beginning to drain away, and the nights to draw in. We missed out on autumn foraging: mushrooms and berries, windfall apples and delicious

Norwegian lobster – anybody's come the first day in October. So high was the excitement at the start of the lobster season that people had been known to stay up to drop their pots until just after midnight on the final night of September, in order to stake the first claim. I so wanted to be part of that. With a nature better suited to autumn and winter, loving fires and hot drinks, crisp walks and trees without leaves, I yearned to experience a Nordic Christmas, in harmony with the season and Småhølmene.

Watching a matinee at the cinema, a documentary on the pianist Glenn Gould, I stumbled on a theory explaining the impulse to go 'north of sixty'. After Gould quit his concert career, he turned to radio, applying to that medium the same perfectionist zeal with which he played piano. I requested the recordings from the sound archives at the British Library where I spent an afternoon listening on repeat to 'The Idea of North', part of his *Solitude Trilogy* broadcast on Canadian radio. Gould argued that man is drawn north by the incentive of uniting there against a common enemy, nature; that, fleeing society, man discovers its inducements. And certainly many great men embarked on hazardous expeditions to Norway and Iceland over the long nineteenth century. One thinks of the pioneer of the Arts and Crafts movement William Morris, the poets Louis MacNeice and W. H. Auden, all tourists of the north. Survival in a cold climate depends upon strong bonds between people, at the 'moral equivalent of war' against the elements. There is ultimate dependence on one's neighbour. Common need breaks down boundaries that exist between strangers in town. I was certain that to overwinter in Norway I would need a friend.

The colder the season, the more it seemed designed for company. It was never pleasant to be long alone on the island, and a solitary stay would be inconceivable in the great freeze. In Lars, Mor-mor had found the perfect island companion. They shared what was essential between them. Meeting Paddy and finding that he fitted Småhølmene perfectly, I had a growing confidence that I had found my comrade. He was also an accomplished daydreamer, susceptible to the draw of what was unknown.

Over the autumn and winter the idea of existence pared down to its essentials, giving a fresh focus, took on huge appeal. After reuniting blissfully, Paddy's and my basement room became more like a dungeon with each passing week. The expectations aired at second breakfasts and in countless letters that the world would spread before us seemed naive and foolish. By November, his usually impervious confidence began to falter. We had long cross conversations in which I was accusatory and then tearful. Paddy had a tendency towards explosions, and I towards sulking. By Christmas it was deadlock.

I slept a lot through the holiday, giving way to exhaustion. Then, slowly drawing strength from food and family, I let myself dream fancifully of Paddy and me on the island, away from the racket of London. What began whimsically, turning over in my mind whether the sea would really freeze, and what it would be like to live there in extreme cold, soon developed into a project, albeit one with a romantic overlay. The fate of Småhølmene in winter had long remained a mystery, and like all good mysteries it eventually roused the urge to investigate. I tried to envision the familiar coast merged under snow and ice, mainlanders and islanders getting around on skates or skis, children digging snow trenches in backyards. Marit's stories of her early marriage came back to me, as I yearned for the sort of winter that would breathe magic and adventure back into life.

As a child, caught up in the bustle of late-summer departure, I had watched, too small to be of use, as the boats were stabled in the boathouse, like horses in from the field, listening to the creaking of the old slipway and the muffled shouting of instructions from inside, where Thomas would be taking charge. My imagination failed to supply any of the tempests that would soon beat against the boathouse doors, and then the dip in temperatures that would still and quieten the storm, making a white and frozen land. I only needed to examine the old house to see evidence of the ravages of winter. The skirting in the sitting-room, the kitchen and Mor-mor's room was all bleached by the marauding sea, a strip as washed-out as the white skin below a plaster.

Paddy and I had time and savings enough to disappear for a few months at least. It would be salvation for us, and a renaissance for the island. It was everything but ordinary, an entirely, wonderfully uncommon idea. It had never been hazarded, and stood against all sense. A chorus of various characters clamoured their disapproval of so impractical a scheme, but I felt only a rising excitement. The Honeymoon room had removed one impediment to a winter stay. With a merry fire in the Jotul, the room was soon snug, and very well insulated. A woodpile, therefore, as well as supplies of food and water, would form the basics required for survival.

January and February, usually such dreary months, flew by as Paddy and I forgot old grievances and instead thought about what to take with us, and how our time might be filled in Norway. We each gave a month's notice period. My only sadness was saying goodbye to the customers who had made life bearable at the oppressively smart chocolate shop where I worked, wrapping Christmas, then Valentine's bonbons and ganaches. I told them I was off to Norway to experience true cold and they wished me well. I could tell they were looking forward to spring, while I wanted the clocks to stay back, not go forward. The chocolate retail calendar, for employees, made the year seem further advanced than it was. By the time I left, I felt sick of all the Easter bunnies and chickens that swamped the counter. Paddy meanwhile had been working in a cheese shop. On his last day he issued a general invitation to his colleagues to visit us on the island. When he told me, it was as close as we came, in the run-up to departure, to arguing.

We would leave early in March and hoped to stay until June. I had no idea how much of that time, over the coldest spell at least, should be given simply to survival, an endurance test against a hostile climate. Early to mid-April signals the start of spring in Norway, much later than in England, meaning our visit would span, over three months, the same number of seasons: winter, spring and the arrival of summer. The prospect was thrilling rather than daunting. I thought carefully about what books to take and bought rolls of film for my manual Olympus camera, a twenty-first birthday present from a sister. Paddy was planning to take his typewriter in the hopes of keeping up a surprisingly large correspondence. His brothers and sisters, scattered around the globe, were all great letter-writers. Paddy also wanted to document his island experiences, and encouraged me to do the same. That these would be worth recording, neither of us had a doubt.

For my sisters, at least, proponents of good sense and personal development, I felt I had to provide the visit with an agenda. I would repaint the kitchen and Paddy would undertake any repairs he could. When we returned, we would try to get our writing published in the travel supplements. Justifiably, there were raised eyebrows when our plan was introduced.

All Mamma's concerns related to the safety of the scheme, endless 'what if's, which kept her up late at night drinking glasses of milk and snacking on comforting mother's mess. She might have been a confirmed worrier, but I gave way to her as a superior authority on the island, so her words had some impact. It took all Paddy's confident and persuasive rhetoric to convince Mamma, and in so doing allay my own fears. He had a special knack for communicating his enthusiasm to those around him. In our time together I had felt the force of this, taking book recommendations, championing his ideas, allowing myself to be directed. Mamma pored over old photograph albums, showing us pictures of Mor-mor's ski holidays in Kopperslan, while I drank in her old memories.

It was as though we were embarking on a long sea voyage as we prepared for departure. Our cases were stuffed with dry food, cold-weather gear and a few treasured possessions. These would be important as reminders of home. Paddy stowed a pipe and acquired pipe-tobacco at Harrods. He filled a leather-bound hipflask with fortifying brandy. Both pipe and flask were presents from his best friend George, to whom Paddy had promised regular letters. From Pappa I had an elegant fox-fur Russian hat and a quilted ski jacket, brought out of retirement, which had useful pockets in the sleeve. We had invested in a wind-up radio. I was as addicted to radio as I was to coffee. An island without either was inconceivable. We lingered in the shop while the coffee beans were measured out, and I found a St John's Wort herb tisane, said to be a natural remedy for the winter blues. That went on tab too. Later I sought comfort in the kitchen and made a whisky-laced fruitcake, anticipating it tiding us over arrival week, while Paddy went out in search of the novels of Knut Hamsun, the feted Norwegian author, whose house stood between Lillesand and Grimstad. He was a local hero in the southlands, as was Gabriel Scott, the great fairytale writer. Both had been members of cousin Sosse's cause célèbre, the Riksmål Society. It was typical of Paddy that his first impulse was to seek out a local author, to learn all he could before setting out.

❋

The night before departure, Mamma made a fortifying supper of baked aubergine and Norwegian apple pudding. Adding to the party atmosphere, my cousin Charlotte, Aunt Anne's middle daughter, made a fourth around the table, doing hilarious imitations of a very croaky Mor-mor. Clumsy with excitement, I overturned a glass. Wine went everywhere but the mood of goodwill prevailed. The telephone rang endlessly, which usually would have driven me mad, and I had to remind myself to enjoy. Parting advice from well-wishers ranged from the practical to the esoteric. Paddy's father, who was a pragmatist, extolled the quality of Norwegian tinned food. Sasha emphasised the importance of exercising to keep blood pumping round the body, experience hard-earned living in an unheated garret over one freezing winter.

There was no time for an extended goodbye in the morning. Mamma stood waving us off in her dressing-gown, crumpled from sleep. Wearing our thickest clothing and shoes, and carrying heavy bags, we were uncomfortably hot all the way to the airport. Spring would soon burst on London. There were sticky leaf buds on the trees and crocuses in the parks.

From the air, Oslo seemed drenched in light, merging sky, land and water. The mountains wore snow hoods. The fjord was a frosted looking-glass. As we stepped from the aircraft, each breath hit the throat like a draught of ice water. Thick snow acted like a silencer. Our bodies reacted with a shock, as though adjusting to a new element. Before I reached the terminal gate my feet had started to go numb. I was also experiencing some inner turbulence. We both felt suddenly very young and unsure of ourselves. Rather than talk of our bewilderment, for fear it would only make things worse, we sought its only true cure: sustenance. We drank cups of hot coffee and shared a prawn sandwich, waiting for our gate to be called. This got up our strength and we boarded the inland flight with fresh optimism.

We were not even to reach Småhølmene on the evening of our arrival in Norway. Peter Widmer, who would become our sage and guru through the stay, thought it best we spent the night at his workshop before setting off for the island the following morning. By the time the bus drove into Lillesand, the light had turned dusky. We missed the stop and had to beg the bus driver to let us off when we realised our mistake, trudging back to Widmer Motor, leaving heavy prints in the snow. My lungs gulped in the new air, my throat feeling hoarse with the cold. Always a quaint town, Lillesand was iced like a wedding cake. It had the ubiquity of a kingdom long ago and far away – like all the towns we had passed, and perhaps all the towns the bus would pass on its onward journey.

Peter had given us a small living apartment above the workshop, which looked out on to the marina. Behind the curtains, the water looked like an ice rink glowing in the moonlight. The sense of our snugness was deeply connected to all that was outside, the cold unable to touch us while we might admire its beauty. I felt then so peaceful and so happy: we had light and warmth and supper to look forward to. Peter was taking us to a restaurant in a hotel, one of the principal buildings of the town. I was eager for the outing, as much for the experience as for the food, of which I did not have very high expectations: I had never eaten there. Ravenously hungry, I chose steak anyway, with all the recommended vegetables. Peter asked for extra potatoes in place of the greens; 'Steak Widmer', he called it. Looking at us critically, he advised our bulking-up. We were thin and peaky after London, comparing miserably to Peter, who was massive and pink-cheeked from a harsh Norwegian winter. He had a sweet tooth and ordered a tray of *linzebøller*, like a croquembouche, filled with vanilla cream, which we were invited to share. As a child I had always considered that the cream choux buns were Peter's one and only weakness. He popped one, two, three into his mouth, swallowing in a single gulp.

The conversation took a practical turn and Paddy tried to stifle a yawn. But gradually, his attention was riveted by a series of astonishing facts. The usual route to the island along the Blindleia might well be inaccessible under a blockade of thick ice, ten centimetres deep in places. This would mean taking the wild, rocky, outer sea route to the island, ferried by Peter. In the morning we must buy rations to last many days, maybe even weeks, for we would be marooned at Småhølmene at least until the summer run-around, with its light 9.9 horsepower engine, could be towed to the island at the first sign of a let-up in the weather. This alarmed me. I hated any loss of independence and a boat was fundamental to my sense of freedom. Without it, we would be deprived of a means of escape, from danger, or even from each other, should we desire it.

Småhølmene had always been a place set adrift from whatever I found unpleasant in ordinary life, and yet I had often used it as somewhere to ponder, to daydream of lives and people, and to problem-solve, so that some dialogue was kept up between the island and the world. And it struck me only while I faced the prospect of complete severance what it meant really to be islanded. My thoughts felt imprisoned by the idea. I would be exiled, outcast and alone.

Snow began to fall very lightly as we left the restaurant. It seemed so benign and soft that I held out my hands, where it landed, tiny flakes that blinked into beads of water. Mamma had given me green-tinted miracle cream to stop my nose going red in the cold, which I blotched on generously before bed. I inherited my bad circulation from Mor-mor, who had suffered from Raynaud's disease and, besides dead fingers and toes, got a blue nose in the cold. Mamma also gave me knitted woollen bed socks, which I pulled on before huddling under the cover.

The following morning, layers of thermals under our clothes, we set off early to breakfast at the bakery on the town square. The sky was cold arctic-blue and our breath came in clouds as we walked along the deserted streets. There were tyre-marks on the road but we saw no cars and everything was very quiet. We sat at a window table drinking cups of black coffee, dipping in bits of bread roll spread with butter and cloudberry jam. A wagtail, emboldened by hunger, hopped about where the snow had been swept in a windscreen wipers' arc before the bakery steps. A scattering of salt lay on the paving, a rather ordinary grubby brown. In contrast to summer visits, when I gladly shed all traces of city life, I was savouring every last moment of civilisation. With reluctance I stood up to go, two heavy loaves of rye bread under my arm, Paddy with a great quantity of poppy-seed *knekkebrød*, useful as it had a long shelf life. He had a pixyish look, with his white face and red cheeks and wild curls escaping from under his hat.

✳

In the famous Norwegian landscape painting of the early nineteenth century – the canvases of Johan Christian Dahl and Johannes Flintoe and the like – tiny huts seem to quake under mountainous cataracts, or villages huddle in the shadowy crooks of sublime valleys. They are a reminder of what it is for man to exist in a hostile landscape, and ask what draws people to live seemingly in defiance of nature, when they must face a daily struggle for survival. But it takes a certain mood to look at them, and to feel empathy for what it might be like to live in such a manner. When in low spirits, the viewer is more forcibly impressed by the austerity of the countryside or seascape. So it was with me the morning of our icy outbound journey to the island. I had never before looked at the Blindleia except in holiday mood. Now, faced with intimations of the Scandinavian sublime, my soul shrank in awe.

Passing slowly through a sea fjord, the engine cut out. The pine-thick hills that dwarfed the boat loomed larger and darker than anything I had ever set eyes on. The trees were not so much green as black, sweeps of shade among the blue-and-grey and white. I felt far away from home and all I knew, so clung to Paddy when he clambered back into *Buster*, eyes shining with glee after testing his weight on the ice. I wondered then what on earth we were doing. Clods of falling snow echoed around the valley. The frozen lagoon was veined with blue inspected close-up. Suddenly everything felt bloodless, fingers, face and feet. As holding a cube of ice can feel almost like a flame in the hand, so the colour the cold gives to the skin looks and feels a lot like a burn. My cheeks were raw and hot. Movement was better than to be still, when the dull ache of the cold became really punishing.

Peter reversed us out of the fjord through the slush and ice cut by the propeller. We turned for the open sea, and islands fled by like departing spirits. As the boat gathered speed, most of all my ears were cold. Freezing wind tunnelled inside, drowning Paddy's voice as he pointed out some place of interest that we passed. The green pastures of Akerøya were all white and ghostly and I imagined our own Raspberry Island would be the same. And yet it was March. I felt deprived without the evidence of spring. The boat slowed and Småhølmene appeared like an iceberg from the deep blue. The sheer compactness of it amazed me. Ice plains stretched out from the mainland as though trying to reclaim it.

The lagoon curled in ink-blue ripples. The old house on its snowy spit looked a picture of subdued charm. The chimney-tops wore white pillbox hats and all the window sashes were powdered, making the panes look darker though not less friendly. There was a drama as I forgot where the keys were hidden and the three of us rushed around trying to locate them. It was as if all my coordinates were lost in the snow. I was slow and unhelpful and Paddy had to chivvy me along. Once we were inside, we hurried around making beds and lighting fires. Peter was giving us lessons in survival, adjusting the catches of the Jotul to show how, starved of air, the logs would slow-burn, emitting heat that would last through the day, and mapping out a diagram of the best pathway to the *brygge* that we must dig the next morning.

Slowly, the Honeymoon quarters started to feel cosy. Warmth clouded the windowpanes to obscure the steely view outdoors. When there was nothing more Peter could do for us, he motored away, promising to return with our boat at the first opportunity. With him gone, I dawdled some more as reference points emerged everywhere from the business of settling-in. There was a neat coin-stack weighting down a Scrabble score with old rivals Becky and Emmie's initials in the margins, and a bundle of dry mussels and crab claws arranged prettily on one of the bedside tables. It began a process of excavation that would outlast the stay, as I sought to root out all that was familiar and thread together summer histories. There was comfort in reminiscence. I glanced up at the *Willing of Jersey*. Though I had never much liked the painting, the loneliness of the ship now struck a note of accord.

I was running through in my head possible menus for an early supper, for not only did breakfast seem a long time ago, but, at Småhølmene, the arrival meal was of the utmost importance. It was, like New Year's Eve, a portal into a new world, setting the tone for future holiday meals. It imposed constraints upon the cook, who had to fit into the bustle of unpacking the preparation of something comforting, yet not overly complicated; to provide a dish to warm and sustain after a long day of travel, while making it part of the winding-down process for herself, and adjusting to the new tempo. A slow-cooked pasta sauce, a store-cupboard stew, a gentle nursery soup: all these could smooth the way.

Paddy smoked an early cigarette and twiddled with the knobs on the wind-up radio, trying to get a signal. When he succeeded, and a BBC voice was carved out of the hum and crackle, he turned the volume low but left the radio playing for background noise. He took out a book of astronomy, saying he was going to learn the names of star constellations, and shelved it and Robert Graves's *Greek Myths* for dipping into over the coming months. I could sense his great contentment as he sat down to read in front of the fire.

The snowy island promised the dawning of a new era of equality between us, since none of my old associations, nor indeed Paddy's from the previous summer, fitted this winter island, making it a Newfoundland, like John Donne's, for both of us. In London, Paddy had been cast adrift. At Småhølmene, his confidence returned, sweeping me up in its flood.

Snow and Solitude

Twenty below was the lowest the temperature hit over our first week on the island. The days were bright and clear but the nights trembled with snow. Sometimes, early in the morning, when it was still dark, the cloud broke and stars appeared above the mainland, glittering over the ice plains. It was the coldest time, the cinders dying overnight, our breath coming in clouds as we crept, like children on Christmas night, to look out of the window at the breaking dawn. Through my bed socks I could feel the floorboards icy beneath my feet, before leaping back under the covers as Paddy lit the first fire of the day, on which we would cook thick porridge to eat with molasses and cream for first breakfast. Norway had countless different variants on this breakfast fuel, from everyday barley porridge to sour cream porridge, thought to be nourishing to new mothers, and served at ceremonies from weddings to funerals. I baulked at topping the gruel with hard-boiled egg and prunes, a traditional dish from Telemark.

Very quickly we had reinstated our second-breakfast policy. We were constantly hungry as our bodies fought to keep warm. Everything tasted wonderful. By eleven, the cast-iron plates on top of the Jotul would be hot enough to make toast, hot enough to have fried an egg, I thought, not quite brave enough to try. I did make rye griddle pancakes though. They were so good, and such a lot were left over, which we ate cold at teatime spread with butter and foamy honey. Norway has a strong tradition of skillet or griddle breads, my favourite being *Skrivarbrød* or 'writer's bread' from Hedmark, 'written on' with a bark comb.

Island toast was a real treat, buttery and singed, cut into soldiers to dip into a soft-boiled yolk, or buckling beneath fruit jam. Paddy's father had been quite correct on Norway's superior preserved foods. The most common supermarket jam was utterly delicious. We gained the habit of leaving our coffee on the fire-stand, keeping it hot and warming the china so that our fingers curled gratefully around the cups. A thick skin formed on the surface of the rich milky coffee and we spooned it off hungrily. The scalding cream top was the best bit, like the skin of the rice pudding. We felt a sense of triumph at what we saw as our ingenuity until, one morning, I put the cafetière down carelessly and it spilt in a riot of hissing and bubbling, leaving me with a badly blistered arm.

There were few signs of life. The outer sea, though free from the ice, was almost as smooth and flat. We frequently imagined we were the only two people left in the world, and our voices sounded louder for the surrounding silences. The birds were our only regular visitors, so all the more welcome. We saw eider ducks gliding serenely through the Gull Channel, and the little wagtails pecking up crumbs where I had swept a breadboard over flattened snow. Two wild swans sailed into the lagoon looking for food. Sea swans had uppity manners, but winter made me kind and I hunted for stale bread to give them, which they sucked up hungrily from the water. Like boats head to wind, the brave great black-backed seagull couple, overwintering on the tiny islands behind the house, faced into the eye of the snowstorms and freezing gales. Through their feathers I could see they were much leaner than in summertime. Their hardiness was breathtaking.

We managed to clamber across the *Kongeveien* bridge and along the left arm of the island as far as Little Beach, where we built a snowman with rowan-berry eyes and rowan twigs for arms. Our tracks were soon filled by fresh snow. So complete were its effects it was like the tide, obliterating Man Friday footprints and flattening sandcastles.

There were just fifty-six minutes less daylight than in London. In the weak afternoon sun, we sat on sheepskin rugs looking over the Blindleia, eating fruitcake with smoky tea and taking puffs of a shared cigarette, blowing steam-engine clouds into the air. By ten past six, the sun sank below the mainland. I would start cooking as the chiming of Big Ben cued in the six o'clock news from London: the hour difference meant that the World Service broadcast was at seven o'clock Norwegian time, so also allowed the pouring of the first drink. There was the clink of ice as Paddy sipped whisky from a tumbler, and thus fortified he strode about the room with a book in his hands, or colonised the table with his typewriter, hammering out lengthy letters. I tinkered around the fireplace, where a bottle of red wine would be warming by the flue, enjoying the smells and sounds as supper took shape.

❄

What finer season than the winter to devote hours to the kitchen? And what better place to bask in the joys of cooking than the island, a place I had always found an inspiration, for all that the galley room was eccentrically equipped, and the gas cooker at times needed second-guessing. Cooking kept me grounded. I was in danger of living too much in the mind, and clung to the physical aspect of it just as I compulsively walked or swam elsewhere. To banish the cold from the old house, and my bones, I was very active and energetic. I divided duties between the old house and the Honeymoon, but I preferred to be in the old house.

There I made simple breads and biscuits, and felt like a proper Norwegian cook, knowing one hundred and one ways to bake excellently. With scarcely any fresh food, and only basic ingredients at my disposal, I grew more resourceful. I was nevertheless easily distracted. Ransacking the store-cupboard for fresh ideas, I found myself lingering over a jar because it brought a recollection that I treasured. I met friends there among the bottles, whose very shapes jogged the memory. And it gave me pleasure to find good ends for the provisions my family stowed away in case of emergency. The store-cupboard was useful at last, like the sail-loft, where the summer timber we were burning for winter fuel was essentially keeping Paddy and me alive.

Cooking over the Jotul stove in the sitting-room, I felt as though I had travelled back in time. It sucked me into the process but also into the past, its heat not conjured out of a bottle of gas or an electric flex. It took me back to what I thought of romantically as the Old Norway. I could adjust the vent to make the logs burn quicker or slower, the contents of a pot boil or simmer. I began to taste instinctively as I went along, something I never bothered to do in London, lifting the prongs of a cooking fork to the tip of my tongue and adjusting spice or seasoning. It was a kind of cooking that drew one in and I became sensitive and engaged.

Rationing was stricter than anything practised in the summer. Perhaps because it was so, Paddy was the enforcer, and not me, though I had been raised in thrift. I could sense him mentally keeping a check of what we got through. Stocks brought with us from London depleted fast. The wedge of Parmesan became a hunk small enough to bait a mousetrap. The plinth of cooking chocolate was soon more like a toe chipped off a great sculpture. I found myself nibbling the store-cupboard's supply of bloomed chocolate to see whether it was still good.

I took care to use only what was needed, never to be excessive, or overly greedy. I became cunning at making things stretch, but also bringing out flavour, lifting our canned beans into a different sphere. I emptied teabags to extract mint or fennel when the dried-herb shelf was found wanting, and whirred spices in the coffee grinder for seasoning. I soon learnt that soda was a safer bet than yeast bread, for the leavening agent perished in the cold. I crossed the loaves superstitiously, letting out the fairies. Miraculously there was never a failure; waste would have been devastating.

In the evening especially I loved to cook. The windows of the kitchen soon steamed up so I forgot to mind that, across the ice of the Blindleia, the coastal houses were deserted. Leaving the lagoon-side door ajar for ventilation, I might spy the lights of a ship on the dark horizon. Housewives are supposed to leave a candle in the window to guide lost sailors home from sea and I followed the practice superstitiously, though it was only to lead Paddy to supper along the dark path from the Honeymoon quarters. I curled up on the faded terracotta sofa to leaf through old cook-books while enticing smells stole out of the most closely lidded dish. In some of the more antiquarian books, I discovered notes and inserts in Mor-mor's hand. I found an old diary, which I tried to decipher, poring over the diction-ary Paddy had brought with us. When I was frustrated by my slowness I became a graphologist, interpreting Mor-mor's character through her writing. It was too scattershot a hand to record anything that was precise.

I imagined rather it listed eccentric triumphs such as banishing day-trippers or putting off unwanted guests.

A fresh loaf of bread was the start of many of our early spring meals. We also consumed large quantities of onions and became very inventive with the uses thereof. Coming in from the snow to Paddy's onion soup with cheese toasts, or spiced rice and lentils topped with shreds of crispy onion, I felt immediately soothed and well cared-for. The perfume of cooking onions hung in the air and sometimes in our clothes. Because all our smells were communal, we did not mind much. Spaghetti sometimes came just with onions, braised over the fire in olive oil and butter, with wild dried thyme, or, more exotically, with tinned sardines and raisins. I marked the first fortnight with Paddy's favourite *spaghetti alla puttanesca*, with olives, capers and anchovies, by which time we were dangerously low on water. News broadcasts on the World Service were transmitting to us the threat of avian flu. Our table talk was on the risks of introducing the pandemic to Småhølmene in melting snow to drink.

❋

Unspoken ritual settled quickly over our days, as we built a routine for perfect existence. Our differences were of only the most incidental and surmountable sort. Paddy preferred his coffee late on in the morning, by which time I had a headache and felt put-upon. But I let him have his way, and then found the time between first and second breakfast was an opportunity to do as I liked, knowing the second innings was coming with its pots of steaming coffee. I sought out nooks where I could bury myself in a book or writing, trailing blankets around with me to be snug wherever I landed. By clearing the sheets and towels from the mezzanine in the washroom I secured myself a library, though one where I could reach out and touch Mamma's work basket, or be reminded of a fond memory by the pattern on a *dyne* cover with Dordie's school name-tape stitched on the corner.

Being in a place well known, with little in the way of novelty or distraction to capture the mind, allowed old memories to stir, sometimes resurfacing in bizarre and rambling dreams. In them, Småhølmene and the tall town-house in Kensington merged, drawing together the two worlds of my childhood. Thinking I had found the door to the lime-tree garden, I was tumbled headfirst into the lagoon and woke with a start. Disconcerted, I immersed myself in the entries of the *hyttebok* as the more solid remembrances from summers past. These diary extracts became like chapters from a novel, peppered with incident and anecdote, drama and action; then I discovered it was not only I, but Paddy too, who in the solitude of the island roved through his past, and through childhood. He always had a new story to recount, tales from Hong Kong where he spent a part of his boyhood, but mainly from Rosses Point, a place which seemed as ever-present to him as Småhølmene was to me when I was away.

The snow was the primary, most essential fact of our present and, lost in its silence and stillness, a feeling of great tranquillity overwhelmed me. Its beauty – the gleaming scabbards of ice beneath the *brygge*, a perfect bank of snow on a window sash – clarified whatever was clouded or unhappy in my thoughts and did a great deal towards simplifying my view of life. So long as we were warm, comfortable and well fed, we were at rights with the world.

I discovered charm in the drowsy buzzing of flies, stirred by the warmth of a fire from their winter sleep, even in the woodlice lying beneath mattresses like war casualties in grey armour. The more I inhabited the past, the more it seemed as though I was communicating with ghosts. The old house, filled with the trappings of Mor-mor, seemed suddenly full of Mor-mor herself. I found myself under her influence. Every time I crossed a sun stripe lining the floor with gold, I sat down within its pool, turning my chin into the sunlight. With the advantage that they required very little space, her Mensendieck stretching exercises kept me limber, and the cold at bay.

Even the living seemed ghostly companions, whispering from far away. Parents, siblings, cousins – anyone who had ever been to the island – I could recall with absolute clarity their island ways. The women of Småhølmene especially were with me as I basked in the history of the place. The island seemed to extol and exhort feminine rule. Paddy did not realise he was outnumbered. But he was, as I harnessed the traditions of the strong women who had made it their business to become mistresses of the island.

I made sure I pulled my weight in the heavy manual work, carrying logs from the sail-loft, chopping the bigger stumps of wood with Pappa's heavy axe, developing blisters on my hands that I showed off proudly to Paddy. I shovelled snow with added gusto, setting my cheeks aflame and getting a frozen shoulder in the process, a second badge of achievement as I saw it. I should have felt like Sisyphus, facing a task that was unending, watching as clouds approached with heavy grey bellies, promising to undo all my hard work. But I found shovelling invigorating, deeply satisfying and hard to stop.

At times I amused myself by thinking of my digging as the desperate bid of a prisoner to escape, turning Småhølmene into a new Alcatraz. The groaning of the sea ice was a key turning in a rusted lock; the snowdrifts were barricades and the great frozen plains protruding from the mainland a prison wall. As prisoners leave their initials on the cell-block wall, so we would symbolically leave our imprint on the place.

The sea temperature lurked around freezing and it could have been catastrophic if one of us fell in out of earshot of the other. I had diced with danger, storming out of the bedroom after an argument with Paddy, getting as far as I could from the house and then crouching like a seal on what felt like an ice floe, with water lapping over my snow boots. Even through my black mood I could see the absurdity of the situation. Paddy was watching anxiously for my return and our relief at being safely reunited brought about a truce.

Feeling dirty aggravated any ill feeling and we took saunas almost every other day, which left us lighter in body and spirit. Paddy was tranquillised by the heat, breathing rhythmically with his eyes closed. The sauna brought out his philosophising nature and I knew he would have plenty to say once we had finished. I battled to still the mind. For me, the sauna was as full of memories as any room of the house, and I longed to tell Paddy stories as and when they came to me. But I tried to hold out, respecting his silence. Watching snowflakes brush against the tiny porthole window gave me an idea. Ice absorbs moisture like a sponge. Rather than brave the sea after the last round, we could rub handfuls of snow over our bodies. It was like putting an ice cube in soda and watching the bubbles cling around it. The snow felt hard, like a pumice stone, and we tottered back dizzily to the Honeymoon. A violent rosiness replaced our former pallor. Instead of dressing fully, which was a battle as everything seemed to fit too well and to have smaller wrist- and ankle-holes sewn in, like a cruel game, we paced around in thermal undergarments, rehydrating with weak tea.

❄

March is recorded in my memory as two distinct epochs: the marooning period and the era of the boat. This latter began with the island loosening itself from the grip of the cold. Icicles melted like licked lollipops into the lagoon. The ice and snow gleamed beneath clear blue skies. On the mainland, tree arms were tinted promisingly with green through their parasols of snow. The seagulls' beaks looked yellower and the birds ruffled their feathers importantly, knowing spring would be coming. I felt robust, fortified by clean air, sleep and food. I trained binoculars over the water, stopping as I came to a flag flying by one of the little chalets on the water's edge. It was a sign of promise, a flickering suggestion of good times to come. By summer, flags ran in a colourful bunting along the mainland, residences modest and grand all equal under the patriotic banners. There was the triangle with a blue-and-white stripe running through a sea of red for common occasions. A larger, rectangular flag with the Nordic cross was reserved for high days and holidays.

Paddy was in charge of all flag duties. He raised ours at sunrise, often wearing just his snow boots. When he returned to bed I was dragged into an icy embrace as atonement for languishing warmly in bed. He lowered the flag at sunset, in accordance with the custom of the country. This daily ritual seemed to satisfy him. It was the one task he had in which I never interfered.

I no longer remembered what day it was instinctively when I woke. Weekends and weekdays melded together. In the mornings I took to counting off the days since we had left London. The end of March was approaching.

I began to long for movement. I was expecting Peter to arrive with the two-stroke 9.9 at every moment. In the end it was Paddy, practising boat knots on a little chair placed outside the Honeymoon-room door, who heard the whirr of a motor first.

Peter brought fresh cardamom butter buns and letters from home. I recognised Mamma's writing, and a Sligo postmark meant one from Paddy's father. A third envelope, with the direction scrawled importantly in royal-blue ink, was harder to identify. Preparing coffee, I tried to guess whom this might be from. In our solitude, news became a commodity – we would share all our letters and, wanting to give proper attention to our first visitor in a fortnight, wait to read them until later. Dipping *bøller* into my coffee reminded me how much I missed things that were unwholesome. Our diet was built of staples, which suited Paddy, who liked interludes of asceticism as a corrective to what he saw as the excesses of city living. But resurrecting old cookbooks I had feasted my eyes on the mouth-watering colour plates – those sinful little cakes my childish appetite had always craved, and my mother resisted, making. I was tempted before Easter to try out the less worthy among them.

Peter gave some basic outboard-motor training before he left, taking me through the procedure for starting. I was always rusty at the beginning of the Småhølmene season. I forgot where the choke was and the angle required pulling the start-lead. The cold made even harder work of things, but I hit lucky third or fourth time round and, cheered by my success, performed a circuit of the lagoon to accustom myself to the feel of the boat's engine. I drew in close against the snowy verges, making full inspection of the empery. The railing of the Japanese Bridge had a smart white ruff, and at the Little Bay an ice floe was getting pushed against a rock by a current.

The boat, our passport to freedom, would allow us to explore the coastline and of course fish. Paddy stomped across to the boathouse wearing a head torch to inspect the fishing nets and trapping pots lying out of action since Mor-mor's day and see what could be salvaged. Worried by his long absence, I went in search of him, and found him in front of the identification poster of north Atlantic fish and shellfish. I thought his ambition spelled trouble, knowing he would not be content with a few plump cod.

I read the letters over. The mystery envelope came from cousin Sibella, Mor-mor's favourite eldest grand-daughter. It came with a recipe for her family *Linzertorte*, which I promised myself to make at the first opportunity. The inclusion of rum in the pastry seemed almost voluptuous, island cookery with abandoned morals. And it would be an excuse for a trip to Lillesand to replenish victuals, since it required much butter and eggs, ground almonds, and more jam than we could spare.

Easter Island

Early one morning, not long after Peter's visit, I woke to see Paddy craning out of the window wearing a jacket over his pyjamas. The grate was empty and his breath was spreading clouds over the glass panes. Wondering what held him so enthralled, I wriggled reluctantly from bed. A chunky white fishing boat lay near to shore. The fisherman was pulling up a teeming eel trap – quite ghastly in its writhing. His black dog stood at the prow, alert as if keeping lookout. The picture captured Paddy's imagination and I could feel him yearning to catch his first eel.

But before he embarked on anything so ambitious – none of my family had ever trapped an eel – I was insistent he accompany me line-fishing to catch our first winter *torsk*. It was a business getting ready. While I ransacked the sail-loft for spare rowlocks, Paddy made a flask of coffee and fetched his pipe-tobacco. I wore Mamma's ski salopettes tucked into rubber-soled fishing boots, wound a couple of scarves around my neck and slotted into the old quilted skiing jacket's useful sleeve pocket Trivial Pursuits cards in case of boredom. We fell short when it came to gloves, and were sharing a pair between us. When snow-shovelling this had been no problem, as usually one of us kept inside while the other was at work. While he started the engine and steered us out, Paddy took both gloves. Then we split the pair, holding lines in our gloved hand, ramming the other deep into our jacket pockets. The sea was flat and our voices carried loudly on the water. Seagulls flocked around the boat. Though they are talismans to the fisherman, we caught nothing.

We had better luck the second trip, when I landed two speckled brown cod. I could see Paddy was discomfited that I had caught the fish, and not he. This set the terms for a competition that would outlast the thaw, and in those early days I kept a mental tally of all the cold-water cod and pollack we caught, though I lost ground fast once he had mastered the nets and pots, bringing in more than we could possibly eat between us. In the southlands, cod is poached in water and served with buttered carrots and potatoes. A slotted fish spoon and fish kettle is the only equipment required, since the vegetables can be boiled economically in the stock. It is a juggling act to get all the timings right, and to make sure everything is steaming hot for the table. But once it is done, the cook can succumb to the wonderful sedative effect of cod prepared in such fashion.

❋

April came and still we kept to our routine, though things were changing so fast that every day brought, as Paddy had anticipated, an event or a sight worth recording. *Little Thomas* emerged from beneath an igloo, upturned on the rocks. Brushing off the remaining snow, I rolled her to the water's edge and, with Paddy's help, into it. This meant exercise and independence because when the sea was flat I took to rowing over to Calvøya to walk across the island. I moored at Calvehagen, Peter's summer house, and trudged through his woods, grateful for free movement. I missed walking far more than Paddy, who though a sociable walker didn't seem to need it for harmonising the mind as I did. I never planned a route, but simply wandered among the trees, marvelling at the shapes the snow had made. I travelled in what I think were wide circles, sometimes fearing I was lost. While I was absent, Paddy would work on the nets or bait a pot for a crab supper. So long as he had this interest I knew he was content.

Meltwater streamed from the mainland, bowling floes of ice out to sea, where they would soon disperse entirely. If I got home before Paddy, I would stoke the fire and cook something for his return. In periods of solitude on the island, I frequently lost myself in tasks that were completely mundane, like sweeping or dusting. Paddy would tell me I had used the time wastefully, and ought to have read. But I enjoyed the ordinariness and domesticity. I liked looking up from a task to see a new bird on the lagoon, or the jewel colours of starfish and crabs in the water. There were often rainbows on the horizon.

I had the radio on for background noise, but was inattentive, immersed in my new world.

The eventless nature of our life then was anything but boring. True to his word, Paddy was keeping a journal. Inspired by him, I found myself doing the same. We shared all we wrote and so found a monitor for every aspect of our island life. In the evenings, as we read aloud to each other before bed, I was reminded of the Viking sagas: an oral tradition passed down between the generations. I imagined our children, then our children's children, reading our island chronicles.

Ties with home were maintained on trips to Lillesand. We walked briskly up the hill to the post office to buy stamps for all our stored-up envelopes, then down again to collect our mail from Peter, who lived by the jetty. He had given us an open invitation to shower at his workshop and we brought little bottles of shampoo and liquid soap in our bags. We habitually read our letters at the bakery. Paddy would stand at the counter and um and ah over the buns and cakes. He was indecisive and asked me for help choosing – was *Napoleonkake* the same as *bløtkake*? And what was I going to have? Selection over, we sat at our favourite table by the window to savour our coffee and treat.

One trip we picked up paint for the kitchen, fulfilling our obligation to my sisters. Paddy and I agreed on a cloudy grey-green, almost the same colour as eucalyptus bark, half matte and half gloss. A sample patch on the wall showed the shade to be only very slightly lighter than Mamma's Le

Creuset kitchenware. By hanging the pots carefully by the handles around the cooker, Mamma had found space for all. It was heavy-duty stuff. As a child I had felt some pride when first strong enough to lift one off its peg for her use. Paddy and I removed each from its position and soon the mattress in Mor-mor's room was piled high.

I discovered Mor-mor's old canvas overalls in the sail-loft. Though much too small, they were irresistible. We worked in harmony, forgetting the time and our aching arms, listening to music with the door open to air the room. I was much slower than Paddy, and took more breaks. Gradually the kitchen re-emerged new and bright. I emptied the store-cupboard, giving each of the shelves a fresh paper lining, and took special care that only what earned its place was put back, making a junk pile to take to the mainland: rusted pliers to break crab claws, chipped plates. It was always sad when anything was booted from the kitchen. My family were senti-mental, me most of all, for I made stories with only shreds of evidence, picking out what I imagined was Mor-mor's favour-ite eggcup or sugar bowl, choosing it as my own best. I took coffee from the same cup every day, convinced it was the one Mor-mor would have chosen. It was pink and smooth as a sugared almond, and felt just the right size and weight in my hand. There was no saucer and I left a trail of coffee rings.

I was sorry when our painting was over and Paddy had hung the last pot back on its peg. Wanting to mark the occasion, I made dough for hot cross buns, sending up a prayer that the dried yeast would work now the weather was warmer. During the first rise the dough swelled into its tea-towel gently, like a hot-air balloon filling with gas. I made thirty or so buns from it and crossed each with rolled-out marzipan strips, balancing the tray beneath the Jotul in the Honeymoon room for the second prove. I watched and waited and nothing happened until, despairing at the prospect of the tough little rock cakes that I would have to bake off, I witnessed them grow like mushrooms before my very eyes.

We ate our feast side by side, propped against the stoop outside the kitchen door. The lagoon had a foreshortened look and the rocks were patchy with the last of the snow. Tufts of coarse grass and heather showed through like stubble. It would have been almost ugly but for the colours, which were vivid under sky blue like a mussel shell. After we had finished I went inside to run my fingers over the glossy walls, inhaling a heady mix of cinnamon, cloves and new paint. The changes happening so fast around us stirred an impulse. I wanted no more washing-up over the stove in our bedroom. No more stuffy indoor lunches, another legacy of the snow. I begged Paddy to help me carry down Pappa's staggeringly heavy, green dining-table from the sail-loft to set beneath the awning on the Blindleia side. When that was done, I took the plaid floor-mats one by one from the old house, to hang over the washing-line. I fetched Mor-mor's carpet beater and whacked them, spreading dust clouds into the air. Then I switched on the fridge.

❋

April is a changeable month. No sooner had I accomplished my spring clean than the winter again seemed to take hold of the land. Paddy sat inside, draining eggs to decorate for Easter. I often stumbled on him absorbed in occupations that were pure Mor-mor: sitting on the floor in a sun stripe, hard at work on some project or other. It would be the first Easter we had spent together, an important milestone for us. It was also my first Easter in Norway. I should have been building myself up for a grand time. But as I prepared for the celebration, family and England were never far from my mind. I found myself longing for word from home, and when Peter came on Maundy Thursday, bringing a take-out supper of prawns in Thousand Island dressing, pulled pork with rice, and a bag of cream buns, the letters he took from an inside pocket as an afterthought were almost more welcome. My parents had written to wish us a Happy Easter, and Paddy had a letter from his father in Sligo, asking if we had killed each other yet; and if not, when we were going to get married, since we had come through what must be the ultimate test.

Enclosed in another letter, from Paddy's sister Sophie in Greece, was a picture, a fantasy desert island with an 'X' marks the spot for treasure and scattered palms drawn by his seven-year-old niece. It was a beautiful misrepresentation of our condition. Sophie, who was a tremendous home cook, had replied to my query on how to prepare *horta* – boiled wild greens – from the young dandelion shoots which would soon pepper all the verges of Høvåg, and also transcribed an Easter biscuit recipe that I could follow using what we had in the store-cupboard. I resolved to make a batch the morning of Good Friday, hoping this would make Paddy feel close to his family and that he was not pining, as I was, after absent friends. Our isolation was like a pact, drawing us strongly together. Not only were we starting to pick up one another's speech patterns, and turns of phrase – which is to be expected living in close proximity – but communication was often non-verbal, as we learnt to anticipate one another in every feeling or sentiment. I dreaded lest he pick up my abstraction, since it made me feel like a traitor to us, and our island state.

That morning, at my suggestion, we also wrote clues for a treasure hunt. Organised fun often annoyed Paddy, could dampen even his sunniest moods, but I hoped he would see this as a tribute to the liberation of the island from the snow, a celebration of our new-found free movement. We lay across the bed, tearing off scraps of paper and scribbling cryptic puzzles. When no obvious prize suggested itself, we agreed to buy one another breakfast at the bakery, a joint reward. Paddy had struck up a friendship with one of the assistants, a pale-faced man, who belonged to a cold-weather swimming club called the Socks Club. Eccentrically they swam naked but for their socks, and Paddy took to enquiring about water temperature each time we visited, working himself up to his first dip of the season. I, meanwhile, had rekindled a friendship with Marit Syvertson, the fisherman's wife, who had worked at the pharmacy in Lillesand for as long as I could remember. This brought our first official supper invitation, scheduled the fortnight after Easter, provided the weather held.

We took it in turns to hide our carefully written clues. Before concealing them I read each riddle through, chuckling over what I had dreamt up and longing for Paddy to find them. The trail led from the boathouse to the second gulls' nest on the far reaches of the right arm of rock, then on to Cornwall, with a final clue hidden in the branches of a rowan tree.

A cold wind was blowing from the south. When his turn came to hide the clues, Paddy, having stripped down to shorts while pruning the rugosas – which had replaced snow-shovelling as a favourite activity – soon had to return to the house to fetch a jersey. Discovering one of mine – a navy-blue Guernsey – before his own, he pulled that over his head instead. We were almost the same size. Many were the shared items and in the mornings often it was a case of first up, best dressed. I pretended to shut my eyes as Paddy set off again but was soon watching his progress. As he nestled one clue beneath a loose roof tile it fluttered away into the sea and he grimaced crossly.

The game was over. I had won and, feeling far from victorious, I was standing in the kitchen window looking out for his return. Paddy's last riddle lay on the worktop and I picked it up and read it through again, feeling his confidence of a win. The kettle hissed to the boil. Emptying too much coffee into the cafetière, I shook some back into the packet, missed, and swept the granules in the bin. Paddy approached from the back with his face set, complaining my rhymes were pretty, but incomprehensible. It took much to salvage good relations.

The bad weather lasted right through Easter. Without the distraction of the snow, the cold penetrated to the very marrow of our being. The wind was cruel and the sky brightened only once, on Easter Sunday, mocking us with a spectacular sunset. Paddy and I had felt tissicky all morning, deciding too late to try to reach Høvåg in time for Easter service. The tolling of the church bells carried over the water, giving us a hollow feeling in our stomachs: homesickness. Our carefully constructed routine broke under it, and we were listless and desolate. Even the gulls were turning their backs, facing crossly into the wind.

We sought escape in a modest foraging expedition to Trondarøya, in search of boiling weeds and fish. On the outward journey I hooked a two- or three-pound cod, enough to feed two: our Easter meal. Covering the bucket with an oilskin to keep the fish out of sight of the birds, we set off on a ramble, exploring the rocky wildernesses. I had a nocturnal poacher's knowledge of the island, acquired as my family and I combed its shores under cover of darkness on midnight crabbing expeditions. By daylight, I became less sure and led Paddy along many false trails. He followed disconsolately, taking swigs of brandy from the leather-bound hipflask when I stopped to pick dandelion shoots for lunch. Our walk was littered with ill omens: an adder slithering beneath a rock, a half-devoured bird carcass. We passed padlocked houses with shuttered windows. The atmosphere became oppressive and we hurried back to the boat, pleased at least that we should not be returning empty-handed.

Sometimes the good of a walk can come from making one extremely glad to be home again. Abandoning all thought of proper lunch we made do breaking off corners from slabs of *melkesjokolade* and dipping them into hot tea, which was far more effective in cheering us up, feeling casual and scratched together. Then we concentrated on supper. Following cousin Sibella's recipe, I made a raspberry *Linzertorte*, feeding the pastry a slug of rum as per instructions. Paddy, in charge of the main course, piggybacked on a lit oven, roasting the cod whole over thick potato coins. He stirred herbs and capers into a mustardy green sauce and picked tiny young sorrel leaves growing around the *brygge* to make into a salad. We forgot to be wistful at the thought of the households abroad devouring plates of lamb and spicy mint sauce, happy to invoke absent friends through our own choice menu.

❋

In most things Paddy was an empiricist; he arrived at conclusions through fact, and I, through instinct. He was always trying to point out to me the names of things – stars, flowers, trees – while I was happiest without specifics, interpreting the world through a private vocabulary of signs and associations. I also refused knowledge I did not like, a habit dating back to childhood, which Paddy, because he was precise, would not consider. I made a mulish pupil. Our methods conflicted most often when fishing, and trips often ended in a quarrel. He needed a hand keeping the boat steady while he lowered his nets, or would have gladly done without me. And I would gladly have stayed behind. I could tell solitary eel-catching, as witnessed from our bedroom window, was his idea of fishing nirvana. Paddy both wanted and needed to learn from a real pro and sought my advice on whether to ask Kay to take him as apprentice on one of his trips.

I wanted to learn the knack of Marit's wonderful *sukkerkake* before immortalising the recipe in the *hyttebok*, so we both had good reason for going to Akerøya. I had pasted in Sophie's Easter biscuits and hoped to make a compendium of tried-and-tested favourites, including ginger cake to warm one in cold weather. The great thing about sugar bread is that, once mastered, it can be used for any number of purposes. It is extremely good plain packed-lunch food. It can be rolled into a jam-spiral or mounted in layers for a *bløtkake*. I envisaged a 17 May cake for us, festooned in Norwegian flags and sandwiched together with thick cream and wild raspberries from the island canes. All this I told Paddy, and our fantasies ran parallel, two streams feeding into the great river of our island vision.

Paddy was increasingly drawn to the idea of self-sufficiency and had taken to spending the best parts of the day in the sail-loft, where he was building a wood-smoker for surplus fish. It was about the size of a large birdhouse, with a hatch door, a wire running at the top from which to hang sides of fish, and a foil urn underneath to contain the cinders. Using juniper and rowan wood, he would make an authentic Småhølmene cure for plumper cod, and, when the shoals came in, for smoked mackerel too. The first firing of Paddy's wood-smoker was not a success. We were alerted from the house by plumes of grey smoke and the smell of burning. The aroma of fish and tar lingered in our clothing, on our hands and in our hair. The cod was rendered completely inedible. But gradually Paddy improved the system to become a master smoker.

When one day we trapped an eel, our first thought was not to eat it fresh, but to smoke it. In bygone times, islanders would home-smoke eels by dangling them down the chimney of the open wood fire using nylon fishing line. I was not willing to allow anything venturesome such as climbing on the curling roof tiles of Småhølmene.

Eels are mysterious creatures, and nothing, not all the books one reads or the stories one is told, prepares for the appalling brutality of killing one's first. Our island specimen lay before us on the *brygge*, oil-slick, giving strong, spasmodic flexes. It could not be lifted up to swipe against a rock, or be kept still long enough to bring a mallet down on its head. A knife-stab threatened to impale the wood or go through my boot, as the blade wavered over the moving target. It was a hateful business, messy and protracted. But at last the eel lay dead, like a spare bicycle inner tube, in a perfect round. As the tube twitched once, twice, an afterlife of nerve endings, Paddy put his hands on his hips and let out a low whistle. He knew that was only the beginning. Next for him was the business of smoking the thing.

The loop of the eel uncoiled from the line and fell to the floor of the wood-smoker. There was a crackle of flame extinguishing. I read belatedly in a tome on fish cookery that the best way to kill an eel was to hit it halfway down its length, knocking out its vulnerable central nervous system, then tried to think of all the nice ways with eel to describe to Paddy, to take his mind off how far wrong things were going: its natural affinity with starchy potatoes, and with creamed horseradish. He looked at me critically and said, 'You think it's too rich anyway.' The skin was coming away from the flesh like a roll of scorched parchment. I gave the end of the fork prongs an experimental lick. At first it tasted just like the other fish we had smoked, though somewhat punchier. Beech and juniper were there, and a blunt fire flavour which came no doubt from its repeated drops into the embers. The fatty deposits around the spine were like pork-pie jelly. Eel was the poor man's meat and we ate poor man's boiled potatoes with it for supper.

It did not compare with the delicious meal of boiled shrimp and beer, with fresh bread and butter, prepared for us by Marit at Akerøya. An expert cook, Marit knew when to keep things simple: fresh from the sea, the shrimp were at their very sweetest. The sight of the fishing boat, moving slowly across the water dredging the seabed, with Paddy and Kay inside, held me momentarily captive at the kitchen window. But soon I was immersed in the business of weighing out sugar and butter for my *sukkerkake*. Marit was a confident teacher, talking rapidly throughout – the cake batter must be put in a cold oven with the door opened not even a peep before the first half-hour was up; the sprinkling of granulated sugar would give the finished cake a delicious crunch. It would not be so easy to make at Småhølmene of course, using scales that were far from exact, and the beaten-up old cake pan. But then all Paddy had learnt would also be hard to execute at the island, where shrimping was something we practised over the *brygge* with plastic-handled nets, to make part of a bucket collage with sapphire-and-emerald crabs and popping weed.

Departure

May came and with it warmth. The world was charged with spring sap. Nesting birds carried thatch in their beaks and the seas were brimming with fish. Paddy and I were privileged witnesses of the changing of the seasons, and the sense of having earned the long, light days made the experience exquisite. The sea thrift was flowering. Cotton grass streamed out from clefts of rock, like sheep's wool caught in barbed wire. I was counting the days until the first mackerel were caught. Paddy, seldom bothering to wear a shirt, was turning what he called 'rufus'. He found jobs that kept him outside, jetting around in *Little Thomas*, or unpicking the fishing nets on the *brygge*. I was allowing myself an idle period before my mother's visit in the second week of May. She, I knew, would have many ideas and schemes for employment.

In the end it was the east wind that saved me from my own inertia. Blowing from sea, it caused a rumpus on the lagoon side that lasted all morning long, while the lagoon itself was showing little white teeth. The white bellies of seagulls soaring over the water seemed almost within reach of the gnashing wavelets. I was desperate for shelter, to have the noise out of my ears. I began to identify with Van Gogh, driven to madness by the ceaseless thrum as I tried to keep up my habit of reading long into the morning. But I found I couldn't concentrate on the words, just the wind, so I began a new project. The coffee table, which had done for all our winter meals, was stained like an old bone and there was just enough paint left over from the kitchen to cover it. I would place it on display beneath the flagpole, drawing up chairs so that we could breakfast outside in style.

I set down newspaper to begin, but progress was slow for distraction lay all around. There were the great black-backed gulls, sharing nesting duties, the handover done, like the Changing of the Guard, with pomp and ceremony. Then an unusual ship's pennant had me running indoors to fetch binoculars to train them over the Blindleia. A window that had been left open upstairs slammed as I came through the door. Running to close it, I remembered film-reel for the Olympus camera, and pirouetted back on myself. The roaring engines of a seaplane taking off out of view drew me irresistibly to the top rock, where I found Paddy, shielding his eyes with a hand and looking up at the sky.

I begged him to work near me, hoping it would help me to channel some of his natural focus. So, to keep me company, Paddy took to sitting at the back, with his typewriter balanced on a stool in front of him. He creased himself into a chair and curled his toes on the baking slates. The clack-clacking of the keys and the shop's bell-ring sound of him starting a new line I found settling. I committed to my work and took photographs of my progress. In the afternoon, the wind softened. Then I too stripped down to my swimming costume, getting so parched and hot that I alternated jumps into the lagoon with cups of strong tea.

❈

May was Mamma's favourite month. The big bleached clouds, the gusts of spray where the currents met and dashed against the lonely skerries, made me think of her and count off the days before she came. I emphasised to Paddy the great honour we were being shown. It was like a monarch coming to a neglected colony, recalling Småhølmene's history and bringing its future again into question. May was a month steeped in the positive and my hopes were high that her visit could bring about a reversal of her plans to sell the island, a course of action she had not absolutely settled upon.

I was not worried about the physical side of her being at Småhølmene again, navigating the rocks and suchlike. She was managing well with the Parkinson's. I never knew her to grumble or to feel sorry for herself. She was a real example. Her sense of humour was keen as ever, which helped her through. What she called 'playing the Parky card' got her out of any number of undesirable situations. Bar the occasional bout of the tremors on her left side, and the little dancing steps she took early on in the morning before the pills kicked in, there were few observable signs of illness. Yet her visit demanded out of the common way that everything was in order. I was desperate for everything to go smoothly, that she might think us worthy custodians; that she might attest to the good we had done for the island through our stay. The smoky grey-green coffee table, spread with the outline of second breakfast – fresh bread, good butter, hard-boiled white eggs and cod's roe – stood beneath the flagpole. A tumbler of Høvåg daffodils, like a brass band, tossed cheerily in the wind. Paddy had carpentered a bench out of drift that had blown in by the Velvet Steps, which fitted two, rather shakily, and an old stool from the sail-loft was resuscitated for a third. There had not been enough paint to match the bench with the table, but the wood had a pleasant washed-out look from the salt. I leant my head back to rest on the rock and squinted into the sun in between sips of coffee. A wagtail sometimes formed part of the ensemble, cocking his head if I stirred, ready to take wing.

Pick-up was at noon and I rowed the Hardanger to Bliksund in good time to meet the car. The boat pulled pleasantly against the current and a light sea breeze countered the heat of exertion. My feet were tanned and I spread my toes to see the white between, listening to the faint trickle of water running along the bottom boards. I stretched out my legs contentedly. I could see they were getting very dry. The skin had a cratered look, like dry earth: a summertime effect. After rowing or walking I had often found myself wanting to swim, slipping in and out of the water like an amphibian. In two-and-a-half months Paddy and I had turned from Inuits to Red Indians.

Long solitude had brought wildness, in both our appearance and our behaviour. I seldom looked in the mirror, but when I did, my eyes danced with new fire. My French bob had grown out and my hair was below shoulder-length. I had cut Paddy's mane with the kitchen scissors, and afterwards watched a bird take a lock in its beak for a distant nest. Mating season was in full swing. On every outpost, courtship rituals were taking place, with much fond neck-pecking. This was followed by a precarious balancing act. Gulls' eggs, which are considered a delicacy in Norway, promised us a valuable source of protein. Feeling it would be taking from my own family, the ransack itself I left to Paddy. I was the getaway driver, waiting in the boat below. I could hear the alarm cry and see the flashes of white as the mates took wing. Then Paddy raced down the rocks, clutching his prize. The eggs were large, a mottled moss-green colour. Paddy scrambled them in grand amounts of butter, which did not quite mask their fishy taste.

I docked the boat and sat, dipping my toes in the cool water and watching the schools of fish, like black darts, until I heard the purr of a car engine. Mamma had of course managed to make friends with the driver over the short journey from Kjevik airport to Bliksund pier. She stayed in the passenger seat, evidently finishing off an important conversation, as I opened the boot and began to carry down the luggage. She had a way with strangers, picking up the loose stitches of a chance encounter and forming a lifelong tapestry of casual acquaintance. As a child, I was suspicious, and as a teenager, infuriated by this habit of hers, especially when she let slip information I considered secret. Now I found it life-affirming, the endless Hellos! and How do you do's? It was part of who she was, perhaps part of who I was, and a far cry from the aloof-sounding Mor-mor, whose stand-offishness had been an embarrassment that Mamma always seemed keen to atone for in endless acts of friendship or charity. Yet when the taxi drove away, and she took in her first view of Småhølmene, letting out a small sigh, it was after all just us again – a family islanded from a life beyond.

She washed off the travel, leaning over the *brygge* and clapping her palms together in the sea, observing from a shade in the water that the Japanese knotweed had colonised the Little Bay – as though she had never been away at all and was merely picking up an old conversation. Admiring the newly painted kitchen, she put London presents neatly on the store-cupboard shelves: lemon biscuits, tea and thick-cut marmalade, with a small bottle of whiskey for Paddy.

Over breakfast, Paddy was eager to recount the tales of the winter, perhaps fearful that this day's sun-drenched idyll seemed all too easy an existence. He fetched the picture from the local newspaper, *Fedreslandsvennen*, taken in early March, showing us standing in a blizzard, which Peter had cut out and saved for us. The ears of my deerstalker are pulled down and Paddy's hair blows wildly around his face. We could be anybody. But the little red cabin is unmistakable even through snow, and this had given us some renown. He told of the trappings of our local celebrity, how we had had strange visitors in the form of woodsmen and fishermen, promising beer and company to keep us from loneliness; that we had resisted their advances, while remaining impressionable enough to agree with one to look round a smart property on a nearby island without getting the consent of the owner, and gullible enough to set a net across the lagoon in the hopes of catching wild sea trout on the advice of another. Paddy told how we had had to beg the harbour master to give us water when the snow began to melt and we no longer had enough to drink, and how he had been persuaded off the island to play football with the local team.

By the early afternoon, Mamma had launched a full-scale assault against the Japanese weed. She stood waist-deep, casting the thick clumps out to sea along the channel where we had caught our first and only eel, the straps of her swimming costume pulled down off her shoulders to give an even brown. In between yanks of seaweed, she turned her face skyward, and murmured, 'Bliss.' She then launched off, swimming towards the lagoon-mouth with Paddy following. They trod water at the border to the Gull Channel, where the bottom shelved away into deeper, colder sea. In late April, Paddy and I had embarked on an inaugural round-the-island swim, when the water temperature was still lurking in the single figures. Paddy, whose ribs were prominent after weeks of rationing and abstention, eating meals his father would describe as 'lav' – meaning very little meat – had deserted at the Velvet Steps. I was euphoric with cold and kept going by a competitive spirit. I wondered whether he would now push on out into the faster water with Mamma as guide.

Paddy and I at this time slept in the old house's upstairs double, a small but significant migration from the Honeymoon room. We left the windows open at night and with the dawn the curtains blew open, letting in the day. Mamma liked an early breakfast and she would often be sitting up as Paddy stripped off for his morning bathe. He emerged gasping mid-lagoon, returning more slowly to the steps. This, like coffee for me, was a ritual without which he was only half awake. We clubbed around the *Kongeveien* stoop, or leant against the sauna door, taking the lead from Mamma.

From sea to plate, our meals relied on teamwork. I was the cook, and Paddy the fisherman, or samphire-picker. The spoils, left in a bucket outside the kitchen, sometimes with a note secured under the handle, reminded me of our university days. I treated each, fresh fish, mussels or greens, as a gift from him to me. The sorrel leaves were no longer pale green, but darker and thicker, a real mouthful in a salad. I washed them carefully, and spun them around my head in a tea-towel, sprinkling a fountain of droplets over the rugosas. I then took out the smartest bowl and dressed them simply with olive oil and salt, sometimes with a splash of red wine vinegar. I loved to watch the leaves begin to wilt on the plate, piled beside something steaming hot from the oven – baked cod in white sauce, or fishcakes. I was also very taken by partnering them with eggs, making sorrel omelettes, fritters and Sunday night favourite, *oeufs en cocotte*. No amount of cooking was too much. I took huge pleasure in my labours, knowing I fed two whose appreciation of my efforts was guaranteed.

Mamma's presence had a domesticating effect. I filled the house with vases of flowers, rowing to Høvåg when I sought something different from the island flora, and collecting wild clover and harebells from the forests. On my rambles I saw much to delight, lusty wild strawberry plants and apple blossom auguring well for the long summer ahead. From a bend in the road, I was staggered by the view of Småhølmene and the outer skerries. The pale islands had turned the columbine-blue water into a lily pond.

I combined these excursions with rubbish runs, as Paddy and Mamma set themselves the challenge of clearing out the sail-loft, both getting very dusty in the process. They flung out paint rollers that had lost their roll and oilskins with long tears along the seams. It was activity of the most improving sort and put them both in a good humour. Mamma, who loved interior restructuring, and constantly surprised at home with a new arrangement of furniture in sitting-room or bedroom, moved books about between shelves. When this was done, she emptied out all the linen and, putting a pile for repairs to one side, got out her work basket for needles and thread.

Had her visit not coincided with the date the water supply was to be reconnected, we would not have achieved half so much. The bathroom in the boathouse was back in action. I carried endless baskets of laundry to hang on the washing-line, where the sheets and *dyne* covers dried in record time because of the wind. Mamma instructed us to fold them 'so that they made "a dried-out undulating thwack", like the Seamus Heaney poem.' She was an expert launderer.

The book reshelving had shed light on overlooked Småhølmene classics. At night-time, Mamma took out *The Oxford Book of Verse* and read through half-remembered favourites. She loved the war poets Wilfred Owen and Siegfried Sassoon, and children's verse-writer Eleanor Farjeon. There was John Masefield's poem 'Sea Fever', which was her desert island poem. I think she felt it encapsulated 'a Småhølmene day', and with that, something of her own spirit, and she pressed me that I insist on its being read at her funeral. The nights were star-filled, and sometimes the three of us sat out on the rocks under *dyner*, eating squares of milk chocolate and planet spotting. The bird sounds always became especially friendly at night.

The seagulls clattered their beaks and the water rippled where a heron that had been fishing in the shallows took wing. An Arctic tern darted on the water, a flash of light like a tiny fish.

❄

I felt melancholy after Mamma left and in need of a lift, so Paddy and I looked forward to the fanfare of 17 May, Norwegian Constitution Day. Here, finally, was a celebration we'd be participating in, and on a national scale. A consultation with the harbour master on the form established that a procession would leave from Høvåg church at ten o'clock, ending up at an elementary school on the outskirts of the town. There, singing, dancing and recitals were to take place. But a longer walk than we bargained for made us slightly late and we arrived in the middle of the mayoral speech.

The schoolyard looked from above like a puppet theatre. Crowds and crowds of small children, like marionettes, were decked out in national costume. They carried tambourines and fiddles, or posies of flowers. Teachers with braids in their hair swept around in heavy dirndls. We had been undecided over what to wear. In the end, we were stupendously underdressed, protected from the drizzle in Mor-mor's felt jacket (me) and canary-yellow oilskins (Paddy). Both of us wore fishing boots. Paddy was unfazed, but I felt self-conscious. I hovered at the edge of proceedings, unwilling to enter the fray. The harbour master rescued us from social exile, introducing us as '*den Engelskmennene*'. Though everyone was very polite, I felt desperately shy. The highlight for us turned out to be cutting a hasty exit with him for a guided tour of the older houses in the village. He pointed out the bay where the bus-boat *Øya* set sail, knew the value of every property, and showed Paddy the house where Gabriel Scott had lived. In the early twentieth century, Svend Holst Jensen, Scott's father, had been parish priest in Høvåg. The tales of his father's congregation, overheard during parish meetings at the vicarage, made a big impact on Scott's storytelling.

At the harbour master's house, a big pot of mutton and cabbage was simmering on the stove. The smell of cooking, though powerful, was pleasantly savoury. Rain now streamed against the windowpanes, and from a window with a sea view I could see the island, looking grey and dismal in the wet. I was in no hurry to get back. That the stew was for the couple's grandchildren, who would come from the school tired and hungry after the festivities, was more a disappointment to Paddy than to me. This, the national dish of Norway, *Fårikål*, is a homely thing, peasant cookery designed to comfort and sustain. Like herring, it harks back to the Old Norway. The slow-cooked meat makes a flavourful broth infused with black peppercorns, and cabbage, a difficult vegetable, is greatly improved from braising in the liquor. Bente, the harbour master's wife, was a cook of the old school with an appetite for the new. She had come to Småhølmene early on in the month for a guided tour of what was edible on the island. This became an information exchange, as she taught me the best way to drain the blood of white fish, or walked with me through the forests to disclose where the best chanterelles would grow come autumn. She had a generous and wise nature, attuned to nature and the seasons. I appointed her to honorary Mor-mor status, or perhaps as my *beste venninder*, best friend and ally. Bottles of home-made jam or pickles found their way to the island, brought by the old harbour master.

Paddy was taken under his wing, as much as I was under his wife's. Paddy and he waged war on local crabs, baiting their pots with devilish adroitness. After I boiled them, I would sit on the *brygge* picking the shells clean, dipping my hands in the sea to wash off the sticky juices. Boiled up, they made fantastic stock. The bisque made its way into Mor-mor-inspired fish stews, fish risotto and paella. I perfected Småhølmene crab pasta, adding fennel seeds in place of fresh herbs, of which we had none. Whilst the spaghetti cooked, Paddy and I sat at the back drinking beer and eating the claw meat doused with melted butter.

Together they caught the first mackerel of the season. The skins glistened richly, like pebbles after the sea has washed over them, and the last-caught fishes leapt as though washing out with the tide. Gutting them, I realised how tiny they were, running the knife easily through their bellies.

Such rich and fatty flesh, which could stand up to fairly robust cooking, would strike a welcome contrast after our winter of cod-eating. Paddy lit the barbecue while I brought down the gramophone and wound it up to play Mendelssohn's *Calm Sea and Prosperous Voyage*. The smells of charcoal and lemon, and the crackle of music, were a new avenue of nostalgia, but also signalled departure.

❉

The last days were astonishingly bright. The wind barely stirred, as if everything held its breath for summer. The water flattened in the still hot days like a sheet under a press. By evening, the sea came suddenly to life, stirred by shoals of mackerel. The fish broke the surface heavily, sending wide rings towards shore. The heron was never far from supper, its silhouette framed against the white dusk of Raspberry Island. The approach of midsummer meant long days and short nights. At all times the land was very silent. In a month, when schools broke up, the crowds would descend. Paddy and I were dreading leaving, but agreed that it would be an appropriate end to our winter adventure. Once the spell of solitude was broken, our dream too would shatter.

We stopped almost all individual projects so as to spend our time together, keeping loosely to our old rituals to give the days structure. We sat at the little table moved from the Honeymoon with breadboards for plates and cups of coffee, reminding ourselves of March meals and how welcome they had tasted. Paddy continued to set his nets and crab pots. If he caught mackerel, we would fry ourselves a late breakfast, more to savour the freshness than because we were hungry. When we needed distraction, we set our sights on gaining our summer badges: swimming to Raspberry and eating a carefully transported picnic there, *kaste sluken* at the Far Rock, and motoring to Brekkestø for an ice cream. It felt different from summer even though the water was warm and the rock scorched the soles of our feet. Real summer was caught up in noise and action.

Our joint *hyttebok* entry was like a testament. Paddy left precise instructions on how to operate the woodsmoker, and where to set the nets, concerned lest his legacies be forgotten. I pasted in some of my own recipes written on to grubby sheets, Sibella's letter with the Easter Linzertorte, the cut-out from local newspaper *Fedreslandsvennen*, and a photograph I had had developed in Lillesand of two home-made loaves of bread. The island kitchen is crossed by a mysterious, diagonal light, like a Vermeer, and it has the effect of making the bread look like a symbol. We agreed on a quotation from Wordsworth, which as soon as it was written I regretted having chosen. Småhølmene would go on as usual after we had left. My sisters were due to stay over the summer, and I had received news by letter that Mamma, such was the success of her May visit, had accepted Sasha's invitation and was to return for a week in August.

I struggled to assess what our long stay amounted to. It had left both Paddy and me feeling deep ties to Småhølmene and, I began to suspect, would compromise the easy-come, easy-go nature of holidaying there in the future. I minded suddenly losing it as the realm of my childhood, a place that was always easy to part with because, whatever happened, we would be back again just the same.

Whatever it was that we were returning to – and if leaving university had presented uncertainty about the future, it was nothing to this – it felt less real than our life on the island. Our absence had left us far behind our friends, who were busy establishing themselves in London and further afield. We sent postgraduate applications to Cambridge and soon A4 envelopes were arriving at Småhølmene bearing official university stamps. We sat outside trying to decode the briefs from funding bodies, weighting down the close-written stacks of paper with stones and coffee cups. The sun on our faces had a muddying effect, slowing the pace of our progress. I had mixed feelings about studying again. To Paddy it was a clever move, once more delaying the inevitable decisions over what to do in life.

We talked of running the island as a seasonal restaurant, open during off-peak months, with me in the kitchen and Paddy ferryman and front-of-house. It was a stunning evening and we were sitting out after dusk. Anything should have seemed possible. But the impracticalities of the scheme were many, and I heard in my head the old family chorus of caveats and rejoinders. We fell into opposition, Paddy the idealist and I the voice of reason, and the conversation ended in an argument.

The island outfoxed all my attempts at serious discussion. Soon I gave up trying to divine what the future held in store for us. When one afternoon the jangle of an ice-cream van carried over from Høvåg, I insisted we row over to try to find it, but by the time we got there it had moved on so we compromised with a walk instead. The dandelion flowers had turned to clocks overnight, and we picked these, blowing the seeds into the air to tell the time. The meadows were full of cow parsley and buttercups. I stopped at the bekeeper's house to buy a pot of spring honey to take home with us.

Our funds were low. The thick wad of notes stashed in Mor-mor's dividable china chicken for security when we first arrived was almost all gone. We blew what little remained on the final trip to Lillesand, buying steak and red wine for our last night. We said goodbye to our friend from the Socks Club when buying a bag of custard *linzebølle* for the Widmers. We left the buns with a note by the door of the workshop, glad not to linger. We were anxious for every last minute of island time. Roland, the caretaker, would drive us to Kjevik airport the morning of our flight. He always spent a week or two on the island at the start of the season, fitting the place up for summer habitation. Between us, Paddy and I had taken care of much that needed doing, meaning he and Marianne could have a restful stay.

On the last afternoon, I swept the house through and made up a bed for them both in Mor-mor's room, filling a tumbler with Michaelmas daisies for the bedside table. Paddy and I were planning to sleep out on the heather, and our bedclothes were drying on the line. After supper, we made our camp on the right arm of the island, above the boathouse. We were expecting a full moon but, in the end, a mist came in from sea, and the night was damp and cold. I woke up before dawn and standing up to shake off stiffness saw the moon, huge and primrose, hanging over the belt of the southlands. The last stars were glowing in the sky. I shook Paddy to wake him up and together we watched the moon until it sank below the horizon, then crossed to the left arm to greet the sun, rising over the outer isles of Calvøya. We swam at the Velvet Steps, and then breakfasted on bread and butter and coffee.

Paddy dressed up carefully for departure. He wore a waistcoat and tie, but with his straggly beard and skinny frame he was still every inch the island castaway. I reluctantly hung up my *lusekofte* cardigan, inhaling the clean woody smell of the Honeymoon room. I then walked into each room to make my farewells. In Norway, it is considered good luck to hide a personal object in a place where one has lived. The old house was full of nooks and crannies from which I could select. The place would keep our secret, the memory of our winter.

❋

Our paths separated in the autumn, as Paddy went off to Cambridge, and I, back to Dublin. He found his subject but I struggled with mine, and remained uncommitted to academia. I became so unhappy that, when a year later I abandoned ship and moved to London, we agreed on the need for a break. Typically, not long after I had left, Paddy returned to Ireland, led by his research interests. We remained close comrades, however, and when I visited him, snatches of the old routine soon found a way in. Paddy lived in a shared house by the sea and kept fairly self-sufficient working on a community allotment. Sometimes he returned from a morning's weeding or digging carrying me a present of fruit, or eggs. Our indulgence, besides the wonderful fresh boiled eggs, into which Paddy dabbed tiny pats of butter so that they melted into the yolk, was to talk of Småhølmene, which we did incessantly. Irish days followed similar patterns to island ones, with walks along the coast to admire wide open seascapes under big skies, or through mossy breathless woods.

I had a strong need for immersion in the world we had given up, because I found that visiting Småhølmene for a week or even a fortnight was, after my three-month term, like being far out to sea in a sailing boat when the wind drops and the sail empties. I could not be happy, could not adjust back to the old summer pattern. I felt I had lost much I had had in common with my siblings. It was an added penalty when I had to face the disappointment of others that Paddy was not with me when I returned, and explain to our old friends in Høvåg and Lillesand why, in all probability, our winter adventure would never be repeated. The harbour master was especially sad, having lost his star pupil. He showed me the barrels of mackerel curing 'sweet and salty' in the boathouse as lobster bait and, for Paddy's sake, I mustered some enthusiasm, knowing how he had dreamt of the autumn fishing. Unsure of my next step forward, I suspected that I required a new set of circumstances in which to make the island my own again. I needed a draught of the new, which would give immediacy to the impressions, and freshness to my vision. The harbour master's wife had given me the key to unlock the forest of all its autumn bounty – the sea then would be teeming with life – and my trusted ally Peter could help me cut wood: September on the island was an idea. And I did as Mor-mor would have done, and returned alone in time for fall.

Thomas was the only family member to have spent time alone at Småhølmene. Before I left, he warned that island solitude can oppress both mind and spirit. Though I took this on board, I embarked enthusiastically. I was sure the island would cocoon me, as it always had done. I took with me provisions and books and prepared for days of repose. I did not let my imagination wander to the night, which would raise ghosts before my stay had begun. I settled into the Honeymoon room and soon had all my things unpacked. I might have felt more comfort from being surrounded by the familiar objects in the old house, but no room there had a lock. On the first night, I slept with the windows shut, though it was warm and stuffy. I burrowed my head under pillows, like Mamma, as if trying to shut out the world, and woke feeling ragged. More nights like it followed, leading not to the sort of pleasant mix-up between waking and sleeping I had experienced with Paddy the hot July after we sat our finals, but a real delirium.

Activities chased on each other's heels, all unsatisfying. I felt tyrannised by mealtimes. Of the two cooks, Mor-mor and Mamma, I had always felt myself to be more like Mor-mor, caring about table settings and how food looked – 'good presentation', as Mamma called it. I found myself entirely unable to simulate her more relaxed approach, and even with nobody to cook for, and nobody to see, I wasted time with lengthy kitchen processes and ended up with meals I had no appetite for and fed most of to the seagulls.

Spiralling into dejection, I accepted an invitation to stay with friends on an island near Risør. We visited the fish market in the town and bought weekend supplies. After supper, I had my first good night's sleep since arriving in Norway and woke feeling eager to explore the new world in which I found myself. I spent the morning swimming and reading and returned to the house hungry for lunch. Being looked after with such kindness, my mind quietened and I gained perspective. I thought back to my childhood summers, how everything had given way to promoting us children's enjoyment of Småhølmene. This gave me resolution. The great adventure of the island was for others to discover, no longer for me. I was ready to let a new generation come forward. I would hand over August birthday celebrations to my nephew Luke, Emmie's younger son, as Great Uncle Alfred had to me. He would anticipate his *bløtkake* with all the relish I remember feeling myself, and claim the marzipan rose.

September 2010

Tills my darling,

Back from supper in the basement to a wealth of family media activity. First a call from Emmie at Småhølmene. The wind was whistling down the receiver and I could hear happy children getting ready to go fishing. Will has told his parents that next year he will go there early and then May will stay on with the Hopes. He is passionate about the place and he and May are over the rocks playing and spying and of course nonstop in and out of the lagoon.

Hope to get time to email you before I leave tomorrow. Meanwhile, lots of love of course and I wish I was in your pocket to make you smile. Your own Mamma

Land Beyond

T he decline of the island without Mamma at the helm to guide activity could only last so long. It was she who truly made the island a place for children, her children, and they now wanted to ensure it remained a place for theirs. What else, where else, could guarantee to make childhood summers so happy? To date, Mamma has ten grandchildren, of whom she is very proud and in whose upbringing she is deeply involved. My siblings have achieved a rare thing, an even distribution between girls and boys. They call her Mor-mor – all except Thomas's two, to whom she is Far-mor. She sews or knits with granddaughters and feeds stodgy nursery puddings or reads nonsense verse to grandsons (her collection of children's books is unparalleled). From her flat in Kensington, the area where she has always lived, a flurry of kitchen activity introduces them to good plain Norwegian food.

The new generation return from island summers with wonderful stories to tell. The rocks toughen the soft soles of their feet, and there is always a stubbed toe or a bruise to show. The Mor-mor gypsy look has been widely inherited, so brown hair is tinted with auburn streaks and their skin turns the colour of milk chocolate. Epic swims, fishing triumphs and competitive kayaking all feed a sense of adventure. But just as important are the everyday things: bailing the boats when it rains; choosing a favourite post-card in the loo; collecting shells on the rocks, imagining each one to be the most beautiful yet. All this gives a happy sense of continuity that keeps our faith in the island, and our will to keep it on, very active.

A routine has emerged that a working party travels to the island on the May bank holiday to take care of repairs and general maintenance. This is usually headed by Thomas, with brothers-in-law to make up numbers, and perhaps a few stray able elder children, or sisters not quite willing to relinquish the traditional female ascendancy.

On one such trip, after lengthy discussion, the sail-loft was converted to make an extra bedroom. Mamma was privy and, amazingly, I felt, had been a proponent of change. But change of the good sort, because an investment in the island's future. From operations headquarters in London, she gave the thumbs-up to the work and persuaded me out of principle opposition. Pre-war oilskins, fishing parapher-nalia, the remainder of Pappa's old carpentry gear and Mor-mor's collection of detective fiction – all were found homes for elsewhere. Jubilant phone-calls were made reporting progress, wind whistling down the receiver. (Mamma's 'head and beard of the troll' is now blotted by a radio mast, giving a strong mobile signal and putting Småhølmene in touch with the outside world at last.)

I ended up being quartered in the renovated sail-loft on my return this summer, since Sasha and her family, plus friends, made it a squeeze to fit everybody in. The weather forecast was bleak, and being set at a distance from the old house was potentially an advantage. Still, I stepped inside with some anxiety. A double mattress had been set in the middle of the floorboards, which were painted a discreet dove-grey. It was plump with *dyner* in the old covers, tied with mismatching ribbons, and quilts embroidered especially by Mamma. Curtains finished off on the old Singer treadle by Sasha were hung only on the day of my arrival. It was a stunner of a room, congruous but separated.

After dark, the whoosh of the wind beneath the *Kongeveien* bridge had the effect of making me feel as though I was in a ship on a stormy sea. I slept very well. When I woke, it was to views often ratifying Mor-mor's point about the island being a microclimate: black clouds over the mainland, and blue skies on the horizon. Some mornings I was pulled from sleep by the shrieks of a nephew or niece leaping into the lagoon. Hamish Olaf, Sasha's eldest child, was turning into a Norseman of the first order. He streaked naked across the rocks and apparently did not feel the cold of the sea, or mind the rain. His friend was always just a little bit behind him, learning the ways of the island.

On the few days when the sun shone over the week, the enticement of a proper *dyne* morning with breakfast on the step soon got me out of bed. Besides, I now felt mistress of the *Kongeveien* strip: my appearance was necessary before proceedings could begin. With our *dyner* slung over the granite, summer reads spine-up as we blinked into the sun, we prepared to be happy. There was the usual tussle to brew enough coffee and to make something deserving of the name 'mother's mess', and then the moment when all was ready, when there was nothing left to do but sit.

The gull chick of Bitte Småhølmene provided children's suppertime with some entertainment, and they were just beginning to feel an attachment to the bird when a squally night did for it. We found the carcass washed ashore among the rubble from the Honeymoon room construction (still no grass), and when Anna, Hamish's younger sister, was told the news, she put on a brave face, and said, 'I'd rather know.'

Unusually all the grown-ups were cooks. We divided responsibilities so that each meal had a different author. I caught cod and cooked it plainly, liking that way better than any other. Sasha was a store-cupboard cook and made delicious post-sauna lunches of warming Janssen's Temptation using superior Norwegian tinned anchovies. It was a dish that needed much love to make on the island, for slicing all those potatoes to such even thin discs without the use of a mandolin or even a sharp knife was very hard indeed. A friend experiencing the eccentricities of the Småhølmene kitchen for the first time, intuitively understanding the frugal principles – which meant every item of island stock must be accounted for – made a delicious dried-mushroom risotto. The soaking liquid made the rice a rich brown, just the thing to warm after a late-night swimming flotilla, and all the palaver of avoiding jellyfish with a mask and snorkel by moonlight.

There was an expedition to Brekkestø for an ice cream and a mammoth row around the sea fjords, with all rowers becoming so hot they flung themselves in the water to bathe. I remained alone on the island, enjoying my solitude, because I knew it would soon end. A harmonious island requires finding alcoves of peace away from the central nerve, the old house. Setting off with chalk in my pocket to draw pictures on the rocks with a nephew or a niece reminded me of how Sasha had led me away on similar pilgrimages. I still had the watercolour she had painted for me, each letter of my name decorated with a picture of a flower beginning with the same letter: thistle, iris, laurel, lily-of-the-valley and yarrow. The pictures coloured by her children, Hamish, Anna and Dora – Norwegian flags, blue lagoons, whales, sea-maids – reminded me of my own early attempts to depict a version of Småhølmene, which were also part realism and part fantasy. These were stuck into scrapbooks or holiday journals, endless pages of summertime.

Some months later, in London, Anna was lying on her stomach on my attic bed rehearsing lines for the school Christmas play. She had her chin in her hands and was flexing her feet to aerial points. 'We would not give it up for all the gold in the world,' she said in best declamatory style. I told her that had struck upon the very sentiment our family felt about Småhølmene, whereupon she danced up and crowed again, 'We would not give it up for all the gold in the world.' I had been lying beside her with my computer on my stomach feeling depressed. The autumn had been draining and I no longer felt I was transporting myself to the island by writing about it. I felt further than ever from goal. How to capture Småhølmene? How to finish the story to leave for my own children, my children's children? Props lay everywhere to trigger one last burst of industry: the illustrated *Norway* Dagmar had given to Mamma; great-grandmother Kiss's *lusekofte* slung over a chair-back; Mor-mor's locket, which had slipped its chain.

My attic room was becoming an island of sorts, cut adrift from the rest of the city, the lights of which I could see twinkling through the skylight at night. I was travelling light, lodging with Sasha to economise and getting to know her, her husband and of course the children in the process. They were hilariously funny, especially little Dora, who coming upon me soaking in the bath with a book, piped up, 'You're living in the bath,' and told her nursery she had an aunt who raced boats in Norway. We were all beset with fears about the safety of their end-of-terrace house, which seemed to be crumbling at the foundations. Long cracks appeared in the plaster almost daily. A panic-stricken Sasha began dreaming of rooftop rescue missions. It was a strange time and one of sympathy and togetherness, for our neurotic preoccupations spelled shared inheritance: Mor-mor.

For three whole years I had kept her character alive in my mind, pulling her out of the shadows, making her friend, grandmother. I had weighed similarities and differences between her and myself, her and Mamma: the three strong women of the story. Now it was time to let go, to unbind myself from their fates and make my own, time to come home to land.

ACKNOWLEDGEMENTS

People say that every first novel is autobiographical. I come from the peculiar position of having built over a scaffolding of fact, the brickwork of fiction. Much of Part I, 'The Settlers', telling the story of Mor-mor, is necessarily imagined. It could not be otherwise, never having known my grandmother. Stories take on new meanings and new emphases over generations; which is to say that though the story is, to the best of my knowledge, based in fact, there have been leaps of guesswork and conjecture. Any faults herein are my own.

Over the three years it took to complete *Island Summers*, I have been given a huge amount of support, editorial and moral, by the exceptional team at Bloomsbury. There are many people to whom I owe thanks, no one more so than Richard Atkinson, who from the first has applied his considerable talent, energy and vision to the project. Put simply, without Richard, I could not have written this book, and I am profoundly grateful to him. The fantastic efforts and input of Phillip Beresford, Laura Brooke, David Foy, Oli Holden-Rea, Nick Humphrey, Natalie Hunt and